AMONG THE ASHES

One pastor's journey with depression

ALFRED LAM

"Fold the worst events of your life
into a narrative of triumph.

Forge Meaning.

Build Identity,
and then invite the world
to share your joy."

— quoted from Andrew Solomon, speaker at TED2014,
writer and lecturer on psychology, politics and the arts

AMONG THE ASHES
Copyright © 2014 Alfred Lam

Email: alfred.lam@gmail.com
Website: www.alfredlam.ca

ISBN: 978-0-9939716-0-0

Editor and Designer: Annabel Middleton

Scripture references are taken from the New International Version (NIV) unless otherwise indicated. Used by permission

Printed in Canada

All rights reserved. No part of this publication may be reproduced, stored in a retrieval system or transmitted in any form or by any means, electronic, mechanical, photocopying, recording or otherwise without the prior permission of the publisher. For rights and permissions, please write to alfred.lam@gmail.com

Contents

Preface   17

Foreword
    By Dr. Philemon Choi Yuen Wan   21

A Therapist's Perspective
    By Diane Marshall   23

A Special Word
    By Brian Childs   27

Introduction   29

Chapter 1
    Shattered Beliefs   39

Chapter 2
    "Daddy, I'm Scared!"   53

Chapter 3
    Dark Night Of The Soul   67

Chapter 4
    "Look, I Make All Things New!"   81

Chapter 5
    A Radical "What If" Community   97

Chapter 6
    We Can Do Better   109

Epilogue 123

Appendix A
When Love Hurts 131
 – A Wife's Journey by Anna Lam

Appendix B
A Theological Transformation 151
 – Daring To Explore My Faith

Appendix C
Getting The Help You Need 163
 – Daring To Ask For Assistance

ABOUT THE AUTHOR

ALFRED LAM is no stranger to feeling out of place. Born in Hong Kong, he came to Canada as a teenager, growing up as one of the few immigrant kids at school.

At 16, he became a Christian but often felt out of place among his peers because he secretly wrestled with doubts and questions about the Christian faith, and simply felt he was not "religious" enough.

In 1988, Alfred graduated from the University of Waterloo, Ontario, with a Bachelor of Arts in Economics. The idea of going to theological college germinated while he was active with the campus Christian fellowship.

As a result, the following year, Alfred attended Ontario Theological Seminary (now renamed Tyndale Seminary) and received his Master of Divinity degree.

For the next 20 years, he served as a pastor at a local church. In fact, he was one of the first English-speaking ministers to be appointed as Senior Pastor of a Chinese church in Canada.

Though his ministry was within the church, he often felt more passionate about what God wants to do beyond the four walls of the church: caring for the poor, being a voice for the oppressed, cultivating healthy communities.

He returned to seminary in 1996 while continuing his work pastoring at the church. After receiving his Doctor of Ministry degree from Gordon-Conwell Theological Seminary in Boston, he spent two years teaching on the subject of preaching at Tyndale Seminary as well as at Singapore Bible College during a sabbatical in 2003.

Yet, despite his academic contributions at seminaries, Alfred always felt that the most important teaching and learning takes place outside the classroom.

From 2005 to 2006, Alfred served as the Chairman of the Board of Directors for Ambassador for Christ, Canada. Yet he never really felt at ease in the boardroom.

When he was diagnosed with depression in 2006, Alfred went from merely feeling out of place to wondering if there was a place for him in this world at all.

Just when it seemed like his entire world was falling apart and his marriage, his family, his career, his health were all crumbling, God began writing a new story for his life out of the chaos and darkness.

Today, Alfred enjoys a new career in the non-profit sector, specializing in collaborative leadership, innovative program development and services for new immigrants.

He still speaks frequently at churches and community events on a wide range of topics – from the reality of living with depression to mobilizing community resources to what it means to live as a follower of Jesus outside the four walls of the church.

As a singer/songwriter, Alfred has also performed in sold-out concerts, raising funds and awareness about mental health. In his free time, Alfred enjoys writing, photography and playing his guitar. You can follow his blog or contact him at **www.alfredlam.ca**.

Alfred and his wife Anna have been married for 22 years, and they live in Toronto with their two daughters, Taylor, aged 10 and two-year-old Mackenzie Jaclyn (MJ).

After years of wrestling with his faith and discovering his true identity in Christ, Alfred is finally *feeling at home*.

Dedicated to my wife Anna, who steadfastly sat with me among the ashes.

ACKNOWLEDGEMENTS

Like any other worthy pursuits in life, the birthing of a book is not accomplished alone. I owe my gratitude to these individuals for turning this book into a reality:

■ To **Diane Marshall** who first planted the idea of a book and faithfully helped me in the writing process, providing valuable insights and feedback along the way.

■ To **Dr. Philemon Choi** for not only agreeing to write the foreword, but for his trusted friendship and encouragement through the darkest years of my life; who never stopped caring for me even as he walked through his own valley of tears grieving the death of his wife.

■ To **Rev. Ka Wong and his wife Jennifer** who put everything they owned on the line for a dream that God had placed in their hearts. In doing so, they taught me three valuable lessons: (1) Dreams cost. (2) Dreams do not always "work out", even though inspired by God. (3) I need to learn to dream again.

■ To **Annabel Middleton** for tirelessly editing this manuscript and designing the "final product". Her magic touch transformed a Microsoft Word file in my computer into the book you are now holding in your hands.

Of course, there are many, many others who have contributed directly or indirectly to the production of this book through your encouragement, words of kindness, and faithful friendships.

There are too many to list here. However, your names will always be "carved on my bones and etched in my heart", to borrow from a familiar Chinese idiom.

Your friendships remind me daily that I am, indeed, a blessed man.

Praise for *Among The Ashes*

Pastors with a Chinese heritage who battle depression live life with a three-fold challenge rooted in shame. Having to function in a role that has high expectations; being born into a heritage that prizes success; and experiencing mental illness in a culture that pursues only happiness – such a combination is a recipe for failure, revulsion and despair.

Alfred has not only tasted these realities, he has written about them transparently without triumphalism, yet with hope, and in doing so, has provided a permission-giving story that will encourage and empower many who are walking the same road.

– Dr. Rod Wilson
President and Professor of Counselling and Psychology
Regent College, Vancouver, Canada

For Christians struggling with mental illness, Alfred Lam's honest account of his experiences sheds light and brings hope. His story gives a glimpse of how it feels to cope with depression.

Among The Ashes is an enlightening book for Christians who are serious about living out their faith. Addressing key concerns raised by biblical writers and Jesus Himself, its challenging messages clearly come from a man who cares deeply that the body of Christ would grow to full stature and the bride of Christ would develop full beauty.

– Rev. Simon Li
Rector, St. John's Anglican Church, Willowdale

In *Among The Ashes*, Alfred Lam recounts his experience of failure, loss and depression honestly, yet without being sensational. The pain and disappointment he went through is shared without rancour, blame or self-pity.

Alfred is also willing to ask the questions raised by his experience without needing to rush to get to the answers. These questions are not merely about depression, but they are really about the nature of the church and its mission. When answers arise, they are relational, not propositional.

Having had the opportunity to walk with him in some small way through this journey, I know this book is born from deep waters and deep searching. That is what makes this a worthy read. One can hope that in sharing his story, others will find the same encouragement on their journey.

– Dr. Brian Craig
Director of Leadership Development
Canadian Baptists of Ontario and Quebec

I have known Alfred for over 20 years. He is someone whom I have always looked up to. In *Among The Ashes*, Alfred speaks from beneath the broken rubble of life – and he is at his best. *Among The Ashes* is painful and beautiful all at once. It speaks the unspoken. It brings you in close to wounds that are raw. Yet ultimately, it releases you back into a world where grace and hope can still be found.

– Lon Wong
Manager of Youth Engagement at World Vision Canada
Founder of unstash.com

For leaders to be effective in the long-term, it is essential that they lead with a healthy sense of well-being, including dimensions of the physical, emotional, mental, relational, and spiritual. Alfred Lam experienced the shattering of these very aspects in his life.

In this book, Alfred shares a stirring and transparent account of his raw experience with depression and painful failures. You will be inspired by his discoveries of a renewed life purpose and a restored sense of wholeness even through the darkest moments of his life.

– Dr. Wilson Leung
Co-Founder
Thinking Forward

Alfred offers a rare, authentic and courageous glimpse into the hidden struggles of depression and pastoral ministry. From the depths of his brokenness comes a heartfelt message of grace, renewal and hope.

This book will not only inspire those with mental health challenges, but it also exhorts the church and communities of faith to deepen their understanding and approach to the gospel of the Kingdom of God.

Though Alfred's story is not yet finished, God continues to rewrite the chapters of his life for His glory.

– Rev. Dr. Kinson Leung
Lead Pastor of English Ministries
Toronto Chinese Community Church

Among The Ashes is a book about one pastor's journey into the hell of depression and back with a vengeance. Alfred's insights and honesty with his faith and his humanity make this book a must-read for those who are trapped in the pit of depression.

> – **Rev. Dr. Herman Chow**
> *Registered Marriage and Family Therapist*
> *Toronto, Canada*

Brutally honest and heart-wrenching, Alfred's painful experience serves as a wake-up call and sincere plea to the church community. This book is not only a rare gift to those who feel cast out, it is also a powerful gift that a parent can offer to a child.

As Alfred writes in his epilogue: "The most valuable legacy parents can leave their kids may lie in how they handle failure rather than in how much they prepare them for success."

As an educator in a society where there is an imbalanced focus on out-performing others, I see the repercussions of a generation that is ill-equipped to face setbacks and failures.

This act of courage in sharing a deeply personal story with the vision of creating a better world is a true legacy for Alfred's daughters and those who long to be understood.

> – **Angela Lee, M.A.**
> *Early Childhood Educator*
> *Hong Kong*

Preface

Depression has a thousand different faces. Each person who suffers from it has his own unique and personal story to tell. Yet at the same time, there are remarkably similar threads that run through our journeys.

I have lived with this debilitating disease called depression for the past decade. I have spoken to many others who suffer from the same illness. It has surprised me to discover that we have so much in common through our silent sufferings – be it battling with bouts of deep sadness without any apparent reason; trying to understand what was happening to us emotionally; hesitating to seek professional help; feeling ashamed about our diagnosis; unwillingness to go on medication.

Whenever I talk about my struggles with depression, almost without exception, the person's eyes will light up at some point in the conversation, as he or she exclaims: "Oh my goodness, that is EXACTLY how I felt. I thought I was the only one!"

When it comes to our personal faith, "rock bottom" experiences in life tend to bring out the best and worst in us – be it in our responses or in our way of thinking.

Some people find their faith further strengthened by the experience while others abandon God as they try to climb their way out on their own.

One of my "rock bottom" moments hit me hard on the first Christmas Sunday after I had resigned from the church.

After 20 years of pastoral ministry, one would have expected to be surrounded by family and dear friends in the familiar environment of a warm church community, especially on Christmas Sunday. Instead, I found myself sitting alone in a McDonalds restaurant, staring forlornly into a coffee cup, exhausted after not having slept for days.

It is difficult to describe the immense loneliness I felt at that time. As I looked around me in disbelief, I actually considered begging complete strangers to just come sit and have a cup of coffee with me…

Through one of my favourite Bible passages, God spoke to me through Isaiah 43:18-19: "Forget the former things; do not dwell on the past. *See, I am doing a new thing! Now it springs up; do you not perceive it?*" (emphasis mine)

> Out of the barrenness of the "rock bottom" places, God had already begun to do a new thing.

Although I could not see it at the time, out of the barrenness of the "rock bottom" places, God had already begun to do a new thing. Like a young plant that springs forth to life from amid the ashes of a forest fire, a new faith had begun to sprout and grow out of my own experiences with depression.

That is what this book is about. On one hand, the book is an account of my story and my journey with depression.

Preface

But it is not a story about the illness. Rather, it is a story about miracles and redemption. It is about love and hope. It is about forgiveness, grace and awakening.

In a world where we so often focus on the things that separate us, I believe it is in sharing our stories that we are brought together.

That is why I want to tell my story – to let those who live with depression know that they are not alone, and to let those who are unfamiliar with the illness know that we are really not that different from each other.

Foreword

BY DR. PHILEMON CHOI YUEN WAN

HON. GENERAL SECRETARY, BREAKTHROUGH, HONG KONG

As I read and re-read the manuscript of this book, I was deeply moved by the personal, honest and humble sharing of my friend and brother in Christ's journey through depression – a journey through the "valley of death".

The themes of each chapter – "powerlessness", "fear", "loneliness" – vividly reveal how painful this journey must have been for him.

Depression can imprison a person to the point of total isolation and desolation. In desperation, Alfred attempted to numb the pain by every method imaginable, including the use of alcohol – without any effect.

I was thus reminded of King David's depression after his sins of adultery and murder. Driven by fear and guilt, King David ran away from God, people and self. He was trapped in utter loneliness (Psalm 139:7-12).

Alfred, too, knows something about this fear, guilt and loneliness. Thankfully, his journey has found a passage of hope with "new wine in new wineskin", as he writes about in this compelling account.

Having been one of the people who had accompanied Alfred along this journey and witnessed his transformation, I can testify to his emerging out of the darkness into light.

During the time I spent with Alfred and his wife and daughter, both in Hong Kong and Toronto, I was touched by the forgiveness and reconciliation which was so deep and truly divine.

Alfred was willing to humble himself and repent, just like King David did when he prayed to God from his valley of darkness:

"Purge me with hyssop, and I shall be clean… Create in me a clean heart, O God, and renew a right spirit within me." (Psalm 51: 7-10).

In *Among The Ashes*, Alfred also shares about his reconnection with his father. Re-united with his whole family, Alfred's story has completely turned a new page.

Renewed by the Holy Spirit, Alfred found the strength to move on. He returned to service for God and for the community in Toronto, reaching out to different ethnic groups with loving hospitality and support.

By God's grace, I believe Alfred and his family will continue to be cleansed and blessed by the Lord – they are a living testimony of His mercy and an instrument of peace to the people Alfred serves today.

May this book be a source of comfort and hope for those who are struggling in the valley of depression.

I pray that this book will also glorify the Lord who redeems and renews everyone who seeks His face.

A Therapist's Perspective

BY DIANE MARSHALL

M.ED., REGISTERED MARRIAGE AND FAMILY THERAPIST,
AAMFT CLINICAL FELLOW AND APPROVED SUPERVISOR,
DIRECTOR, INSTITUTE OF FAMILY LIVING

It is not often that a therapist has the privilege of journeying with someone who has the courage and integrity of Alfred Lam. He was referred to me when he became depressed while ministering to a large multi-generational Chinese congregation.

We worked together during and following the painful period of Alfred's soul-searing confrontation with himself, his subsequent meetings with his fellow pastors, his public confession, resignation, and ultimately, leaving the church which he had loved and served for so many years.

I also met with his wife Anna, a woman of remarkable love and forgiveness, who was willing to work at rebuilding her marriage and begin anew (read her heartfelt account in Appendix A, "When Love Hurts – A Wife's Journey").

Both of them have given me permission to comment on this unique experience of not only being a therapist, but being consulted on the writing of this excellent book many years later.

It is their desire that *Among The Ashes* not only records their journey, but that it will be a source of blessing to clergy of all denominations who find themselves suffering from the depletion and depression of vocational ministry burnout.

Alfred has described the anguish of his breakdown and moral failure with sensitivity and yet with clarity. Too many people in Christian ministry are afraid to face the shame and rejection which Alfred had experienced, and so refrain from being honest – with themselves, their partners, their friends and their colleagues.

As a therapist, I am privileged to witness the different ways – both small and large – in which grace broke through in Alfred's life as he courageously engaged in the painful process of self-examination and truth-telling.

When brokenness and betrayal are present, the path to reconciliation first has to go through the wilderness experience of facing temptations (from lying and deceit to avoidance and blame) until one comes to a place of genuine repentance and openness to reconciliation.

Alfred and Anna have both made that journey and were surprised and blessed in so many unexpected ways. Truly, their story is a testimony to God's unfailing grace!

In *Among The Ashes*, this deeply personal account is not just about a life lost, but about *new life gained*; not just of a status and vision destroyed, but a *new status and vision embraced*. We read about the challenging process of how new wine is able to be poured into new wineskins.

The heart of the matter is grounding in God's love – even if only faintly perceived: the "inner voice of Love"

A Therapist's Perspective

that Catholic priest and author, Henri Nouwen, writes about in his own journal of recovery from clinical depression.

Alfred, too, heard that "still small voice" even when engulfed in the thunderstorms of his pain, shame and grief. Having let oneself down – as well as one's life partner and one's community – is an overwhelming personal tsunami.

Alfred had the courage to face those losses and rebuild his life, step by step. His is a story which will hopefully inspire and encourage others to do the same.

A Special Word

BY BRIAN CHILDS
LEAD PASTOR, THE BRIDGE

A "new thing" is what *Among The Ashes* is all about. This book is about hope and the future – a future that is seen through the learned lens of past experience.

As I read Alfred's book, I found myself drawn into the depths of his pain and yet also up to the heights of newfound joy – and all the many levels in between.

Among The Ashes is about penetrating grace and how the human spirit can be touched by God's Spirit, even in the darkest places. It is about depression – that debilitating, relationship-changing, soul-sapping, life-deadening illness.

But... it is not just about depression; it is about Alfred and his faith. It is about a distinction between our faith in God and our experience with His body, the church.

What bubbles up from these pages is an indomitable spirit – Alfred's. In him lies a spirit that expresses resilient hope, while having lived through painful disappointment.

The stories and encounters that *Among The Ashes* takes us through are vivid, memorable and even a bit haunting.

They leave an indelible mark.

Story after story, Alfred brings us to a place of reflection, to a place of wanting more – from his struggle to get out of the car to brave picking up his medication for the first time; to running alongside his daughter's bike as she expresses fear; to his heart-wrenching public confession of personal failure; to the phone call from his father; to the moment in which he encountered an armless beggar in Bangkok, with his own hands unable to grab change out of his pocket, because they were so full.

Wanting more is a key theme in *Among The Ashes* – more from self, from others, from the church, from God. The wanting has its roots in our brokenness. The radical "What If" community that Alfred introduces us to is a rallying cry for more – more inclusion, more grace, more love, more appreciation for diversity, more belonging.

"We can do better" is the cry from Alfred's heart.

Alfred's experience as told in *Among The Ashes* takes me to my own. Like Alfred, I too, have suffered from the debilitating illness of depression. This honest book acts as a clarifying mirror in many respects.

Reading Alfred's book challenges me to translate my own pain into some kind of gain for others. It leaves me wanting to build a legacy of getting up whenever I fall. It inspires me not to give up, but instead, build an example just like Alfred is building.

That means staying in the fight, running the race, keeping the faith – right to the end.

Introduction

I started writing this book in the midst of the worst ice storm in the history of Toronto, Ontario, Canada. After two days of relentless freezing rain, the entire city became encased in ice. Hundreds of thousands of residents lost all heat and power in their homes for days. We too, had to abandon our home. With two young kids in tow, it was an adventure to say the least.

The timing could not have been worse. The storm hit just days before Christmas – right when the city was about to kick into high gear with festive shopping, parties and all manner of celebrations.

Businesses that counted on Christmas revenues faced deep losses and even bankruptcy as they could not open their shops without power. People scrambled to stock up on supplies. Stores were sold out of everything from road de-icing salt to batteries for flashlights. Insanely long lines formed at gas stations as people feared that the city would run out of fuel. It was something right out of a Hollywood disaster movie script!

* * * * * *

Before the storm, I had drawn up a detailed schedule for my Christmas break. Naturally, all those plans ended up being frozen (pun intended!) with the ice storm.

There was a time when I would have freaked out if anything or anyone derailed my plans.

There was a time when it would have been a disaster of Old Testament epic proportions if we had to cancel (God forbid!) Christmas services.

Instead, I found myself quietly enjoying the additional time I got to spend with my family. Instead, I found myself assuring my wife and daughters:

"It's OK. Everything will be fine. We are safe and we are together – that is all that matters."

That is when it occurred to me: my priorities have changed. *I have changed.*

* * * * * *

Depression changed me. It changed the way I viewed myself. It changed the priorities and values by which I now make my choices and live my life.

Interestingly, as an unexpected by-product, depression also changed *my faith* in a deep and most profound way.

I had been a pastor for nearly 20 years when I was first diagnosed with depression. The illness took its toll on my physical, mental and emotional wellbeing.

Outwardly, I desperately tried to hold up the fragile house of cards, but inwardly, my private life was spiralling out of control. I was heading towards a total annihilation of everything that I had built in my life.

It all started with occasional bouts of sadness which became violent weeping spells that would hit me with no warning. I could be out running an errand or simply walking through a shopping mall, and all of a sudden, I would sit down and weep uncontrollably for no reason.

Every moment I was awake, a deep emotional and physical pain kept stabbing at my heart. I was constantly in pain. I wanted it to go away and did whatever I could to stop the incessant ache. The episodes became more and more frequent, progressing to suicidal thoughts.

One evening, as I was driving down the highway, a transport truck pulled up next to my car. The random thought hit me:

> I stopped caring whether anything I did was "right" or "wrong".

"If I just steer my car a few feet over to the right and drive into the truck, the pain will go away."

It took all of my willpower to refrain from turning the steering wheel towards the transport truck that day. It was only much later that I realized I desperately needed to seek medical attention, which ultimately led to my diagnosis.

Meanwhile, as the depression and the pain got worse, I feared I could only hold up the external façade for so long. I knew that I needed "help". Unfortunately, I went about it in all the wrong ways.

In my attempts to quell the pain, I stopped caring whether anything I did was "right" or "wrong". I just wanted it all to stop. The pain was not just in my head; it was actually physical in nature.

Often, it felt as if someone was sitting on my chest and preventing my lungs from taking in air, while driving a dagger into my heart at the same time.

The first "help" I tried was drinking. I naively thought that I could numb my mind with alcohol. It was the most readily available painkiller I could get my hands on.

Throughout the day, the pain inside was constant and relentless – and it only became worse at night. Before I went to bed, I drank until I could not feel anything anymore, before collapsing into merciful slumber.

When even alcohol failed to numb the pain, I turned to pornography. For me, the attraction of pornography had nothing to do with sex or eroticism. Rather, it held out the false promise of intimacy as an answer to the loneliness in my soul. Pornography offered a make-believe world where pain is magically replaced by pleasure, where physical intimacy comes free with no strings attached and no evident consequences, so to speak.

> Pornography left me feeling twice as empty as before.

Naturally, it was not long before I discovered that none of it was real. Every time I turned off the computer, instead of feeling fulfilled, pornography left me feeling twice as empty as before.

Neither did I have the kind of connections or money to get into drugs. It was a good thing that I did not have such resources, or the outcome might have been much worse.

Introduction

When neither alcohol nor pornography delivered the relief that I so desperately craved, I did something that I, never for a million years, would have imagined myself capable of doing: I had an affair.

Looking back, those choices not only failed to heal my pain, but each of them was actually cutting new and deeper wounds into my soul. I could not see it at the time, but in reality, I was merely masking one pain with another.

After ending the brief affair and admitting to my alcohol abuse, I ended up resigning from my position at the church. After a painful and devastatingly disappointing separation from my church, I found myself at rock bottom – with no job, no idea whether I would ever get better, no assurance that my family would stick with me after what I had done… and no hope.

* * * * * *

Even before my struggle with depression, I had already been wrestling with deep-seated doubts concerning my own faith. As a pastor, I privately questioned whether our conventional "North American" or "Western" interpretation of Christianity was fundamentally missing the point when it comes to understanding what it means to be a follower of Jesus. (See *Appendix B, "A Theological Transformation"*)

In wanting to challenge the congregation to think more deeply for themselves, I began to raise those questions in my sermons from the pulpit. Not surprisingly, I encountered two diametrically opposite responses.

There were those who told me how I gave voice to the very same questions they had been struggling with.

Conversely, there were those who could not accept the notion that their pastor was expressing doubts about some of the commonly held beliefs within the church.

More than a few of them came to me and told me that I needed to "repent" of my ways before I "shipwrecked my faith" and "took the church down" with me.

Little did I know it at the time, but my experience with depression would provide the perfect soil for those seeds of doubt to blossom into a new faith and a fresh understanding of what it truly means to follow Jesus.

* * * * * *

That is my other reason for writing this book – to provide a platform for us as Christians to consider together some important questions as we seek to believe more deeply and genuinely, with a faith that is bolder and bigger, yet at the same time, more humble and gracious.

Here are some thoughts to consider:

What if our traditional understanding of "The Gospel" is incomplete or inadequate?

What if we still have yet to understand fully who Jesus is and what He wants to do in the world today?

What if the church was meant to be something quite different from what we have been accustomed to?

What if we have been too narrow in our understanding of the Bible?

Introduction

My experience tells me I am not alone in wrestling with these questions.

As is the case with embracing anything new, we will not be inspired to consider change unless we are convinced that the old ways are not working anymore.

In Mark 2:22, Jesus talks about putting new wine in old wineskins: "And no one pours new wine into old wineskins. Otherwise, the wine will burst the skins, and both the wine and the wineskins will be ruined. No, they pour new wine into new wineskins."

The reason why old wineskins cannot hold new wine is because new wine is still actively fermenting and will continue to expand with gases, while old wineskins have become inflexible and cannot be stretched to contain the required fermentation process of the new wine.

> **Old wineskins have become inflexible and cannot be stretched...**

In the same way, like the new wine in old wineskins, I realized my newfound faith no longer fit inside the old institutional religious structure in which I had spent most of my adult life.

As my understanding of the Christian faith was being stretched by these new questions, I realized that the old institutional religious structure – which I had been a part of ever since I had become a Christian – was no longer able to stretch with me in my new growth and continue to nurture this process of "fermentation".

There has been plenty of dialogue on what it means to be a "new kind of Christian" (a term created by one of my favourite authors, Brian McLaren, in his book *A New Kind Of Christian*). McLaren is a pastor and one of the leading thinkers in a contemporary movement of Christian thought commonly referred to as "Emergent", which gives voice to the questions many wrestle with concerning what it means to be a Christ follower in this post-modern era.

However, while we have focused on the meaning and nature of this "new faith" – that is, the new wine – there has not been nearly enough discussion on the new wineskin – that is, the community and structure that are required to hold the new wine, so the new faith can continue to "ferment" and nourished to grow and blossom.

I hope somewhere along your reading of this book, we will dream new dreams together about what this new wineskin – this new kind of community – will look like.

* * * * * *

In the movie *The Passion Of The Christ*, one scene showed Jesus carrying the cross through the streets of Jerusalem. He was beaten, bleeding and struggling to make His way to the execution site. His mother followed from a distance.

When He finally collapsed under the weight of the cross, she rushed to His side and said to Him, "I am here."

As He lay there on the ground, Jesus reached out and touched His mother's face. Looking straight into her eyes, He said, "Look, mother, I make all things new!"

Introduction

As I watched that scene over and over again and thought about those dark times in my life, I had a vision and epiphany of sorts.

A transformation began to take place. I saw myself in the scene, in the place of Jesus in a strange kind of juxtaposition: beaten, bleeding, my body ripped, struggling under the tremendous weight of depression.

> **He whispered into my ear: "I will make all things new!"**

When I finally crumbled to the ground in helplessness, unable to take another step, I heard Jesus' words ring out: *"I make all things new!"*

It was then that I realized Jesus was not just talking about some sort of cosmic renewal when He uttered those words – He was actually speaking about *me!*

Christ entered my life when I was completely broken, hurting, beaten, bleeding, crushed… and He whispered into my ear: "I will make all things new!"

* * * * * *

That, above all else, is the message that I want this book to bring to you. If there is nothing else that you take from *Among The Ashes*, just hold on to hope and remember this: *you can be made new.*

Interestingly, in the Bible, those words were not spoken by Jesus on the way to the cross, as portrayed in the movie.

Instead, they are recorded in Revelation 21:3-5, as the writer describes the glorious future that awaits us:

> *"And I heard a loud voice from the throne saying, 'Look! God's dwelling place is now among the people, and He will dwell with them.*
>
> *"They will be His people, and God Himself will be with them and be their God.*
>
> *He will wipe every tear from their eyes.*
>
> *There will be no more death or mourning or crying or pain, for the old order of things has passed away.'*
>
> *"He who was seated on the throne said, 'I am making everything new!'"*

Verse 5 then says:
"Then he said, 'Write this down, for these words are trustworthy and true.'"

* * * * * *

That is why I decided to write this book. May the words that follow bring you hope and remind you that despite all the darkness and brokenness you may be feeling at the moment, the tears will stop, the pain will cease – and most importantly, *you will be made new.*

CHAPTER ONE

Shattered Beliefs

"Somewhere between my unanswered prayers and the realization that I could not worship myself into happiness, my faith died."

– MONICA A. COLEMAN, ASSOCIATE PROFESSOR, CLAREMONT SCHOOL OF THEOLOGY, IN *LOSING FAITH, FINDING HOPE: A JOURNEY WITH DEPRESSION*

I remember vividly the moment when I was diagnosed with depression. I was in my family doctor's office following a near suicide attempt which had left me frightened and confused.

That was when my doctor said to me: "I believe you are suffering from depression, and I want to put you on an antidepressant medication."

Actually, he said a lot more than that, but the only two words I heard were "depression" and "medication".

Even today, it is still difficult for me to put into words the torrent of emotions that flooded over me when I first received my diagnosis. While I did not feel hopeless like a patient who has a terminal illness might, I did become overwhelmed with a sense of foreboding and confusion.

I knew very little about mental health at the time.

Even though I had been a pastor for some time and had done my share of counselling, I had no idea what it meant when the doctor said I was suffering from depression.

When I heard the word "medication", all I could think was: "This must be serious."

My doctor tried to assuage my concerns about the antidepressant medication. I had a flurry of questions:

Will it have side effects? Will it become addictive? Will I grow dependent on it? Will it make me... feel better?

"Medication is only one part of an effective treatment plan for depression," was my doctor's non-committal reply. "There are many variables and we will have to be patient."

Despite his best efforts to answer my questions and provide clear information, all I could see was this thick, impenetrable fog around me. I felt as though I was sitting alone in a boat on a vast lake, shrouded by an opaque cloud that had enveloped me. I could not tell which was the way back to shore. It was a most crippling concoction of uncertainty, loneliness and confusion while facing a frightening unknown future.

In a daze, I mumbled my thanks and stumbled out of the doctor's office with more questions than answers.

Once outside, I found myself on unfamiliar territory. For someone who always had everything under control and always knew what the "plan" was, I did not have a

Chapter One: Shattered Beliefs

plan for this. I did not even know what to do next. *Should I call people and let them know? If so, who should I call? Should I call my parents? Or my wife? Or my friends? Do I have to tell the church? Do I need to tell anyone at all? Should I take some time off? Should I go home? Should I go back to the office?*

On and on swirled the plethora of questions that flooded my mind as I reached into my pocket for my set of car keys. Instead, my fumbling fingers found the prescription slip that my doctor had written for me.

Yes, that was it – I should go to the pharmacy and get my meds. The little slip of paper provided the first sense of direction that I needed since I received my diagnosis. Little was I prepared for the next wave of emotional turmoil.

> **Little was I prepared for the next wave of emotional turmoil.**

I parked outside the pharmacy, turned off the ignition and looked at the prescription slip that I held in my hands. For some inexplicable reason, a paralyzing wave of shame washed over me.

While a patient who has cancer might feel like he or she has received a death sentence, this prescription for an antidepressant felt like a printed declaration of my failure:

I could not "cut it".

I was "mentally weak".

Somehow I had failed.

I sat in my car for what seemed like hours. I did not want to go into the pharmacy. I did not want to be seen with the prescription. Worse, I did not want to risk running into someone from the church and have to lie if they asked why I was there.

When I finally summoned enough courage to get out of my car and approach the prescription counter, I felt as though every pair of eyes in the store was looking at me. When the medication was ready and the pharmacist gave me the instructions on how to take it, I thought everyone around me was listening. I felt so vulnerable and exposed.

As quickly as I could, I paid my bill, grabbed the pills from the pharmacist, hopped into my car and then sped off, pedal to the metal, head hung low.

To this day, I still cannot fully explain the deep shame that I felt then. After all, a diagnosis of depression is not a moral or ethical failure. Even though I had very limited knowledge of depression at the time, I had read enough to know that one in four adults suffer from a diagnosable mental illness, so I knew I was definitely not alone.

Desire For Power

On hindsight, I realized the shame I had felt was rooted in – of all places – my faith and belief system. It was a belief system that was fatally flawed. It had never occurred to me that I was living my faith in a paradox.

Even though I had always believed the Christian faith is one built on grace, in reality I was practising my religion from a position of strength, or more precisely, *power*.

Chapter One: Shattered Beliefs

Many of us claim to take grace seriously as a doctrine, but deep down, we do not think we need grace ourselves. Grace is the insurance policy that we turn to – only if all else fails, but power is the currency that we collect to make sure we never need to cash out on grace.

When we hear the word "power", we naturally think of key leaders in Washington or big people on Wall Street who lust after fame, fortune and influence. From the movies, we have become familiar with its stench.

> **Grace is the insurance policy we turn to – only if all else fails.**

Ironically, the desire for power that has crept into our belief system is much more subtle than that. It is often invisible and odourless. It is hard to detect. It is easy to succumb to. It is literally the devil's "oldest trick in the book".

Remember Eve when she was first tempted in the garden of Eden? The temptation to eat the forbidden fruit was not to become smarter or more beautiful or to live longer. Rather, the devil went for the jugular and tempted her with ultimate power instead: "When you eat (of the fruit from this tree)... you will be *like God*" (Genesis 3:5).

Power – the ability to be in control, to be like God – was the first and most dangerous temptation ever presented to mankind. Since those first opening pages of the Bible, God has been trying to teach man not to succumb to this craving for power.

Yet, that struggle is not limited to past stories of the Bible. It is still very much alive in us today.

In my case, that desire for power manifested itself in seemingly harmless attitudes and beliefs that I had held since the day I became a Christian.

Being Right vs Being Wrong

I had a self-centric faith that was built on what I was able to do and depended on me *being right*.

That included making the *right* decision to "accept Christ" to embark on my faith journey; making sure that I had believed *rightly* before I was deemed qualified for baptism; being examined to determine that I had all the *right* doctrinal positions to become a pastor; and even more tests and examinations to make sure I had all the *right* answers as I prepared to be ordained.

As a young Christian, I was even told that when we ultimately arrive at "the gates of heaven", God will ask us one question and one question only, and it is only by providing the *right* answer that will allow us to enter.

Being right was all that mattered.

Being One of "Us" vs Being One of "Them"

An obsession of being "right" almost always produces a nasty by-product: contempt for those whom we deem to be "wrong", and an unspoken smugness that we are not one of "them". Without realizing it, my brand of faith had created a black-and-white world that separated all people into two camps: "us" vs "them".

Chapter One: Shattered Beliefs

There is "us" who have it "right" – and there is "them".

We are the ones who have gotten it "right" about God and everything else, and will be spending eternity with Him in Heaven. It is up to "us" to convince the rest of the world of their "wrong" ways and rescue "them".

Therein lies the ultimate seat of power – when you divide the world into two sides, and you are convinced God is on your side, it is hard to top that!

This attitude is precisely captured in Jesus' story about the Pharisee and the Tax Collector, as told in Luke 18:9-14:

To some who were confident of their own righteousness and looked down on everyone else, Jesus told this parable:

"Two men went up to the temple to pray, one a Pharisee and the other a tax collector. The Pharisee stood by himself and prayed:

'God, I thank you that I am not like other people – robbers, evildoers, adulterers – or even like this tax collector. I fast twice a week and give a tenth of all I get.'"

Some of us may have the impression that the Old Testament Israelites had to fast all the time. The fact is, the Old Testament law only legislated one day of fasting out of the year. This is held on the Day of Atonement, the most important day in Judaism.

The problem with the Pharisee's prayer is actually not in the showcasing of his piety and religious habits – even though I am sure there was a healthy dose of arrogance that accompanied those words.

In fasting twice a week, the Pharisee demonstrated his commitment to his religion – above and beyond what the Old Testament required (which was just once a year).

Fasting twice a week – or 104 times a year – meant this Pharisee went beyond his religious requirement by over 100 times!

Not only was this Pharisee serious about his religion, he put his money where his mouth was. He said he gave a tenth of all he earned. Technically speaking, his behaviour was exemplary. In our modern church today, he would most likely have been considered by the leaders and pastors to be the model church member!

> We have a tendency to say, "Boy, are we glad we are not one of *them*."

No, the Pharisee's problem did not lie in his piety or financial generosity. Rather, his problem was in the very first thing he said to God as he got up to pray:

"God, I thank you that I am not like other people..."

Or, more precisely, in his attittude: "God, I thank you that I am not one of 'them'."

Haven't we ourselves, when we read the Bible and look at characters like the Pharisees, also have a tendency to say at times, "Boy, are we glad we are not one of *them*!"

I have since gained a new appreciation for the timelessness of the Bible. Most of us think the Bible paints for us characters such as the Pharisees in order to warn us: "Do not be like them."

Actually, I think the Bible presents them as a mirror for us – to show us how much *like them* we truly are.

Jesus And The Powerless

Reading through the New Testament led me to discover that Jesus loves those who are powerless. Jesus loves "them" even when they are unsure of their faith – or even if they do not believe at all anymore.

I am reminded of the story in Mark 9, about a father whose son was sick. In acknowledging his lack of faith, the man cried out: "Help me overcome my unbelief!"

Besides those who struggle with their faith, Jesus also loves those who are too weak to keep up with this power-driven world and have been cast aside, such as the blind man (see Mark 10) who begged from the side of the road: "I want to see!"

I also discovered that Jesus indeed loves "them" all – the desperate and the downtrodden – be it the father who wrestled with his unbelief, or the blind man who desperately wanted to see.

In my parallel journey, I found myself powerless like both the desperate father and the helpless blind man – unable to believe, unable to see.

Looking back, what scared me the most about being diagnosed with depression was not the illness itself, nor the medication. Rather, it was the fact that I was losing my ability to think straight – and in that process, I was losing my confidence in being "right".

For the first time, I felt "powerless".

I feared that I had become one of "them".

Yet, ironically, it was precisely this same fear that led me to perhaps the most important discovery in my spiritual life. In a bizarre twist, as I feared becoming one of "them", I finally grasped the fundamental truth that every child has been taught in Sunday School:

Jesus not only loves them; Jesus loves *me*.

Trusting God vs Playing God

Every weight-loss program and self-help guru dangles the same carrot in front of the audience with their tantalizing message: A New You!

What an attractive notion it is to become new again. However, what most people do not realize is that, in order to "become new", you must first let go of the old. For most of us, that is a very difficult thing to do.

Of course I wanted what Jesus was offering – I wanted to become new. What I did not know was that I had to stop trying to do it my way.

After I had gotten over the initial shock of being diagnosed with depression, I conceded that I needed medication and counselling.

But my mindset was to get it over with as quickly as possible. I did not like the powerlessness that I was feeling. I wanted to be "healed" quickly so that I could

Chapter One: Shattered Beliefs

get back to being who I was before: totally sure of myself, confident of being right and assured of what I believed in.

But God had other plans. I was confronted with what would ultimately be the most fundamental question in my journey towards a new faith. At the end of the day, do I want a faith that is built on trusting God? Or do I want my own version of "faith" that is all about me "playing God"?

Since the first temptation recorded in the Bible to the present-day church, our desire to "play God" or "be like God" has not diminished. But when Jesus came, Philippians 2:7 says He "made Himself nothing".

> Do I want my own version of "faith" that is all about me "playing God"?

He emptied Himself of power.
He embraced sinners.
He touched lepers. He healed the sick
He fed the hungry. He served others.
He washed the feet of those who would betray Him.
He gave up the power to defend Himself.

Finally, when He spread his arms out on the cross and died, He showed mankind once and for all: "This is what it means to play God."

That is what depression ultimately taught me as a Christian. My desire for power – to be right, to be in control – fundamentally keeps me from understanding the way of grace that Jesus offers.

When I could no longer rely on my own power, for the first time in my life, I fully realized my need for grace.

Messed Up Folks Like Me

Going back to the story of the Pharisee and the Tax Collector in the Bible, Luke 18:13 records that the tax collector had "stood at a distance. He would not even look up to heaven, but instead, beat his breast and said 'God, have mercy on me, a sinner.'"

It is evident that tax collector wanted to make amends for his wrongs and make peace with God. So he had gone to the temple to pray.

What I have always found curious is this: how did the tax collector know to "stand at a distance", and not go near or enter the temple?

Most tax collectors in Jesus' day were Jews recruited by the Romans. Naturally, many considered them to be working for the enemy and they were hated by their fellow Jews. However, as a Jewish male, this tax collector could have just entered the temple. It would have been *his right*. Yet he stayed away.

What prompted him to not go near? Who told him? What gave him the idea that he did not belong or was not welcome in the temple?

Here is my theory: perhaps the tax collector stayed away from the Temple for the same reason that so many stay away from the church today – by looking at the people inside!

They look at the people in church, they look at *us*.

Chapter One: Shattered Beliefs

They see the images that we try so hard to put up for the world to see, and they say:
"That is not a place for messed-up folks like me. That is a place for good people – people who have good lives, good jobs, good friends, good marriages, good kids. That is not a place for messed-up folks like me."

* * * * * *

My journey with depression made me truly recognize and admit my need for grace. Grace erases the line between "us" and "them", and in doing so, frees us to be honest about our weaknesses and relieves us from the pressure of trying to not be like "them".

Looking back, depression shattered my life in more ways than one. While I had initially looked at my diagnosis as a declaration of my failure, I now see that it was a road sign along my journey that says "Wrong Way".

It forced me to make a "U-turn", and head towards the right direction of being made new.

CHAPTER TWO

"Daddy, I'm Scared!"

*"If someone has a hundred sheep and one of them wanders
off, doesn't he leave the ninety-nine and go after the one?
And if he finds it, doesn't he make far more over it
than over the ninety-nine who stay put?
Your Father in heaven feels the same way.
He doesn't want to lose even one of these simple believers."*

– MATTHEW 18:12-14, *THE MESSAGE*

Last summer, I experienced an important moment with my older daughter Taylor who was eight years old at the time. It was one of those "rites of passage" in parenthood for me and marked a milestone that fathers and daughters would reminisce about years later: I took the training wheels off Taylor's bike and taught her to ride on two wheels for the first time.

Before allowing her to hop on the bike, I talked her through it countless times. I put so much protective gear on her that she was practically bullet-proof. I made her repeat a hundred times:

"Head up, eyes forward... Pedal! Pedal! Pedal!"

But when the moment came, none of that mattered.

Perched on the bike, she looked up and down the path, then clung onto my arms for dear life and cried:

"Daddy, I'm scared!"

I did my best to reassure her, but like any kid riding a two-wheeler for the first time, she wanted me to hold onto the bike and then run alongside her, even after I had let go.

I am happy to report that Taylor eventually learned to ride without any catastrophic injuries. Neither will I forget the pride in her eyes when she finally managed to make it to the end of our street on her own.

* * * * * *

As I reflected on my own journey of faith with depression, I kept going back to that summer day. In particular, I felt a deep longing to become more like my daughter.

How I wish that, during my worst and darkest days, I had had the honesty to look into the eyes of my faith community – the way my daughter had looked into mine – and plainly admitted: "I am scared."

For as long as I can remember attending church, I had been taught that fear is the antithesis of true faith. Fear is something to be defeated and conquered.

As a Christian, I was supposed to be "strong and courageous". Possessing any fear was not only wrong, but it would displease God, I was told, and the only way to please God was by overcoming those fears and having complete faith in Him.

Chapter Two: "Daddy, I'm Scared!"

However, when the diagnosis of depression dropped in my lap like a death sentence, fear was no longer just "another popular sermon topic" – it became very real:

"What if I never come out of this?"

"What if I can never trust my mind again?"

"What if I end up being locked up in a psychiatric ward for the rest of my life?"

"What if I will never again amount to anything other than a mental illness patient?"

Depression was like a cement block tied to my feet, dragging me deeper and deeper under water, while fear was the demon that encircled me, taunting and laughing at me, all the way down.

Part of my motivation for writing this book was the discovery of how my old way of faith simply did not "work" when I struggled with depression. Faced with the crippling and ever-present fear, all the clichés, slogans and sermon acronyms that I used to draw from in my "bag of tricks" did not help. I did not know how to "get stronger", become "more brave" or grow a "stronger faith".

> Depression was like a cement block tied to my feet, dragging me deeper under water.

Simply put, I did not know how to "just don't do" fear.

In hindsight, I realized what I needed was not a shot of strength or courage, like some sort of steroid injection to my heart. What I desperately needed was to be able to look into the eyes of someone the way my daughter looked into mine that day on the bike, and simply admit "I am scared." Scared of what depression meant. Scared I could not hold it together. Scared of what might befall me.

I needed someone to hold me up when I could not keep my bike upright and straight. I needed to lean on someone, knowing that someone would not let go.

Craving Intimacy

Depression taught me an important lesson which has become a part of my "new faith". That is, the antidote to fear is not faith, bravery, courage or strength; it is *intimacy*.

In my old way of believing, I was taught to simply "be tough". Be brave and face my fear with courage.

While outwardly I put on "bravado", yet inwardly, I secretly craved the kind of intimacy that I could not find – and as a result, I ended up looking for it in all the wrong places, in all the wrong ways.

All addictions – I have since learned – have at least part of its source in a deep inner craving within the soul, a deep hunger for intimacy.

The idea of intimacy with God as a spiritual discipline is certainly not new. In fact, not too long ago, touting the whole idea of "intimacy with God" was actually somewhat "trendy" in the evangelical church circles.

Churches would form small groups to specifically study the subject and "practice" intimacy with God. The rationale usually goes something like this:

Chapter Two: "Daddy, I'm Scared!"

"As Christians, we have paid too much attention to 'doing' as opposed to 'being'.

"As a church, we have become so busy that we have crowded God out of our lives. God does not just want us to do things for Him; He wants us to know Him.

"So, as a church, we will learn to 'do less' and spend more time practising intimacy with God..."

As a pastor, I too, have organized my share of similar campaigns at church. We ran small groups which studied the same curriculum on cultivating intimacy with God.

For some weeks, we even deliberately suspended all meetings and programs, and encouraged people to just come to church and practice extended times of silence and prayer.

We taught and encouraged people to practice fasting as a spiritual discipline in order to draw closer to God.

Can you see the irony in this picture? Looking back now, the paradox is so evident: we were so busy "frantically" trying to "slow down" in our attempts to develop intimacy with God.

> We were so busy "frantically" trying to "slow down"...

In our religious attempts to "stop doing things for God", we ended up simply... *"doing" something else!*

For myself, those "efforts" did not produce the desired results of enjoying intimacy with God – and I am sure I was not the only one who felt that way. From my experience, those well-meaning campaigns rarely produced any lasting changes to speak of.

This begs the "elephant in the room" question no one has dared to ask out loud: "How come it did not work?"

I believe the answer lies in the question itself. They did not work because in the end, that was all it was: *work*.

What Makes A Real Relationship

Pastors often like to illustrate the idea of "working" towards greater intimacy with God by comparing our relationship with God with our romantic relationships. We are told that, in the same way romance with our spouses needs work – be it going on dates, constant communication, thoughtful gifts, spending time, and so on – it takes work to build up our sense of intimacy with God.

It all sounds so reasonable, doesn't it? I myself have probably used the same illustration in my own teaching when I was a pastor.

In re-examining my theology today, I realize there is a fundamental flaw with that illustration – which may explain why all our concerted efforts to "work" towards intimacy with God fail to be effective.

You see, when we talk about working towards closer intimacy with our spouses, we presuppose that there is an existing relationship. We know our spouses. We can see them. We can touch them. They are a living and breathing

Chapter Two: "Daddy, I'm Scared!"

entity in our lives. They are as real as we are. When we make an effort to build intimacy with them, we receive immediate tangible feedback: a smile, a touch, a hug.

The problem with carrying over that concept to a God whom we cannot see and talking about "working to build intimacy with God" is that many of us simply do not have a real relationship with Him to build from in the first place.

The Bible makes it a point to show us how people's relationships with God often begin with a personal and unmistakable encounter with Him. From Jacob, Moses and Elijah in the Old Testament to Paul, Peter and the 12 disciples in the New Testament, each of these men have had a personal and unique encounter with the Lord. No two encounters were alike.

Their stories may be different, but two common themes run through them: in their encounters with God, there was no mistaking that they were meeting with Him; and secondly, it was God Himself who relentlessly pursued them and initiated contact.

> We are used to "programming" people's "response to God".

In contrast, we are used to "programming" people's "response to God". We organize evangelistic campaigns that feature charismatic speakers and impressive theatrical productions. At the right time, we dim the lights, and with moving music playing in the background, we ardently invite people to "respond".

The question is, what exactly are people responding to?

We ourselves have been programmed to present the gospel as a series of concepts or ideas – all designed to show people the "transaction" that needs to take place in order for them to have their sins forgiven and get to heaven after they die.

If people are receptive, they respond in much the same way they do at a car dealership when they decide to accept the deal on the table. So they begin their "Christian lives" by accepting the deal.

Other times, we present the vision and plans we have for the church, and we invite people to become a part of it. Quite often, we will take advantage of opportunities like that and we say something like this:

"Some of you here this morning have not yet accepted Christ into your lives. Here is your opportunity to do that, and become a part of this vision. You can invest your lives and make a difference in this community and the world."

Again, if they are receptive and respond, they will begin a "Christian life" by signing up for a worthy cause.

"Programming" Responses To God

In our evangelical brand of Christianity, we have an incessant need to program, strategize and control just about everything we can think of.

We set numerical targets for how many new believers we want to baptize in a year.

We set goals for growth in attendance and giving.

We lay out three-year visions and five-year plans.

Chapter Two: "Daddy, I'm Scared!"

Best-selling books have been written on how to get everyone in the church to come on board so that we will all share the same vision, buy into the same program and engage in the same process.

Such a "systematic" operation actually works wonders in the fields of manufacturing, production and customer service, where consistency is a must. This kind of thinking discourages anything – or more importantly, anyone – from deviating from the plan or program.

> **He customises His methods and finds creative ways to approach each person.**

Here is the problem: when it comes to the ways in which God chooses to reveal Himself and encounter people, the Bible shows us that He is not exactly consistent.

In fact, God seems to make it a deliberate point to *not* be consistent. Instead, He customises His methods and finds creative ways to approach each person.

He spoke to Balaam the prophet through a donkey.

He used a whale to get Jonah's attention.

He whispered to Elijah through a gentle breeze.

He came to Moses in a burning bush after a 40-year wait in the desert.

He appeared to Paul in a great light and blinded him for three days before calling him to preach.

If there is one thing their encounters with God had in common, it is this: God decided when and how it happened.

It was unpredictable.
It was mystical.
It was spiritual.
It was inconsistent.
Yet it was unmistakably God – and that genuine encounter with God forever changed the person's life.

In our systemic and organizationally driven way of thinking, we do not like things that we cannot predict. We are not comfortable with anything "mystical" that cannot be clearly explained or neatly packaged in a box.

So, in our attempt to make sense of it all, we try to "program" them out of our plans. Instead, we set up our own process or strategy to "make it happen" for people.

Starbucks Coffee claims they do not just sell coffee, but they offer the "coffee house experience". Similarly in the church, we try to strategize how people will come and "experience" God. We do this by running a seeker service, then a visitors' group, then a membership and/or baptismal class... you get the drift.

> We set up our own process or strategy to "make it happen" for people.

We move people through our system like students advancing through a set curriculum, and at a predetermined time in the process, we challenge people to "accept Christ".

I have often wondered, how does a person "accept" a Christ whom he has not personally "encountered"?

Chapter Two: "Daddy, I'm Scared!"

Moreover, if that encounter has not first taken place (at God's initiation, not through a program), exactly what – or who – has the person accepted?

Missing The Main Ingredient
It is not my intention here to go into a lengthy discussion on the merits of church growth methods. However, I am sharing this because this approach to the Christian faith and this way of "doing church" has had a direct bearing on my own experiences and ensuing struggle with depression.

As I mentioned earlier, when I was faced with the fear that accompanied my depression, I longed for intimacy rather than a stronger or more courageous faith.

> I longed for intimacy rather than a stronger or more courageous faith.

I longed to be able to openly admit that I was scared.

I longed for a God who was real and near. But without the intimacy and assurance of an authentic relationship, I discovered that I did not know such a God.

At a young age, I had agreed with the ideas that were presented to me as the "gospel". I never saw the need to question it. In the same vein, I was inspired by the vision of the church to change the world.

In fact, I discovered later on that I had certain skills which made me a suitable candidate for employment in the church. So I made serving the church my lifelong career.

All those things were good, of course, but looking back, something was missing. I was missing the main ingredient: *I had never had a personal encounter with God.*

About 10 years into my pastoral career, I enrolled in a personal spirituality course at the local seminary. At the first lecture, the instructor asked all of us to simply spend 30 minutes in silence, imagining ourselves simply resting in God's embrace.

Afterwards, everyone in the class was able to share what that experience had felt like to them – but not I. The entire exercise had felt alarmingly foreign to me. I had felt *nothing*.

> It was a clear warning signal that there was something vital missing in my soul.

At that time, I dismissed it by saying things like that were simply "not my thing".

In retrospect, perhaps that in itself was a clear warning signal that there was something vital missing in my soul.

The God Who Pursues Us

In our evangelical churches, people who do not "fit" nicely into our strategies, programs and culture often gradually fade away into the background and then eventually walk out the front door altogether.

Sometimes, we may feel it is more "convenient" to let them go. I know I have been guilty of that myself when I was a pastor. It was not until the tables were turned, and

Chapter Two: "Daddy, I'm Scared!"

it became more convenient for everyone else to let me "go away" that I realized how painful it is to leave and not have anyone chase after you.

When I read the stories of men and women who had "messed up" in the Bible, I noticed a pattern. While we find it easier to let people fade into obscurity rather than go after them, God does the exact opposite.

While churches may find it more "convenient" to move forward while leaving behind those who do not fit the mold, God pursues them.

He does not "move forward" without first running back after them.

He reaches out even when they are not aware of their need for Him.

He hangs on to them - and He refuses to let go.

* * * * * *

This was exactly what my daughter needed from me when she had become scared in attempting to ride the two-wheel bike for the first time: the assurance that I would hang on to her and not let go, no matter what.

What my daughter was looking for when she was afraid was akin to my own heart's cry.

What I needed most when I was deep in the valley of fear, I found it in the God who pursued me to the depths even when everyone else had let go.

Never before have I found this familiar passage more personal and fitting:

"If someone has a hundred sheep and one of them wanders off, doesn't he leave the ninety-nine and go after the one?

And if he finds it, doesn't he make far more over it than over the ninety-nine who stay put?

Your Father in heaven feels the same way.

He doesn't want to lose even one of these simple believers."

– Matthew 18:12-14, The Message

CHAPTER THREE

Dark Night Of The Soul

*"You have taken from me friend and neighbour.
Darkness is my closest friend."*

– Psalm 88:18

It was a Sunday in late October when I announced my resignation from the church. At that time, absolutely every aspect of my life was crumbling into pieces. I was no longer physically, mentally or spiritually capable to continue on as a pastor. Resigning was clearly the only and best option for me – and for everyone else.

The cold came early that year, almost as if it was intentionally matching the winter season in my soul. Our church held three services and I announced my leaving, in three languages, to each congregation.

That day was unspeakably painful for me. It felt like I was attending my own funeral – except I had to bury myself three times. In many ways, it *was* a funeral. It was the death of my dreams – and the death of the only life that I had known for almost 20 years.

I struggled through making the announcement in the three services. Each time after I finished, the pain was so intense and unbearable I had to step outside.

Between services, I walked aimlessly in the cold. I wandered on the empty streets near our church building, hoping in vain that the cold would somehow numb the pain that was piercing my soul.

From time to time, the blinding wind picked up the snow and ice, swirling them around and hurling them at me, it seemed. They felt like countless tiny daggers that penetrated my clothes and cut straight to my heart.

As I looked around the deserted streets, I could not remember ever feeling so utterly alone in my life.

After I had made my final announcement, I walked to my car and drove away alone. As the church building – and the only community I had known for all these years – slowly disappeared in my rearview mirror, the painful reality sank in: "From now on, you are on your own."

* * * * * *

Contrary to popular belief, time does not heal all wounds. However, while time may be a lousy healer, it does serve as a wonderful teacher.

Now, years removed from that cold day in October, I have learned that my hopes and dreams did not die that day. Despite how it felt during those low moments, God had never stopped writing my story. He did eventually lead me to discover new visions and dream new dreams.

However, when I look back, I am still somewhat perturbed and pained by what happened.

Two questions in particular deeply trouble me:

Chapter Three: Dark Night Of The Soul

After having dedicated practically every waking moment for almost 20 years of my life to building a community of grace, how is it possible that I ended up so utterly and completely alone at a time when I most needed a community?

As much as that question still pains my soul, it is the second question that scares me the most:

Will I ever be able to entrust myself to another community again?

A Perspective On Pain

Of the chapters that I have written so far, this one proved to be the most painful one to write. In my preparations for the content of this chapter, it was necessary to look up some old emails and correspondence that had taken place between me and the church's leadership during that tumultuous time in my life.

I had simply wanted to refresh my memory on a few things – but as I re-read some of those emails, I suddenly felt an anxiety attack coming on. It was as if the whole experience of personal rejection was brought to life all over again. My heart raced, I had trouble breathing and I had to turn off my computer right away.

Even though I had left the church by choice, in the process I felt rejected and abandoned in ways that I had never felt before – and hopefully never will again.

I wish I could say that I am 100 percent at peace with the past, but the truth is, in revisiting and writing about what happened, I had to search the depths of my heart and make a conscious decision not to rehash what had happened all those years before. There was no point in reliving every word and action – what was said and done, and by whom.

Suffice to say, it was a tremendously difficult time for everyone involved. We all had our reasons for saying and doing certain things. I am sure I had said things that were hurtful as well. I am in no position to judge who was right and who was wrong.

For practically all my adult life, I had preached about the church being a community that is marked by traits like grace, love, acceptance, support, forgiveness, among other virtues. Yet, the irony is that during those darkest hours of my life, my experience with the church ended up being the source of my greatest pain.

We can be better than this.

We *have to* be better than this.

A Perspective On Friendship
One of the most painful experiences after my resignation was how people made it a point to distant themselves from me. Sadly, they included colleagues in the ministry whom I had been friends with.

My wife and I were having lunch in a small diner one Sunday when I noticed a couple seated at the table next to ours. We knew them quite well as a ministry couple from another church.

It was a small restaurant, and the tables were set very closely to each other. I mean, I could have easily reached out and touched the man sitting at the next table.

Chapter Three: Dark Night Of The Soul

As I was about to greet them, I noticed that they were making great efforts to "not notice" my wife and I. You would not believe how hard they worked to "not notice" us. The situation would have been quite funny if it had not been so hurtful.

They leaned away and spoke to each other at a 45-degree angle, facing away from us. They literally buried their faces in the menus and took an unusually long time to pore over their dining options.

When they finally placed their order and reluctantly handed their menus back to the waitress, they ran out of places to hide.

> You would not believe how hard they worked to "not notice" us.

When I reached out to say hello, I did not know whether to laugh or cry at their attempts to act surprised. The small talk lasted for about 20 seconds and then the awkward silence returned.

Mercifully, the food arrived quickly, and he ate like a famished man who had not seen a morsel for months. They finished eating in record time and hurriedly left.

I could go on and recount several other similarly humorous and hurtful encounters. After I got over the initial shock and hurt, I noticed a rather disturbing pattern: it was the most matured Christians, those who had been in the ministry the longest, who were the coldest to us.

What was especially hurtful was the way my wife Anna (who had done nothing wrong) was abandoned right along with me. No one stood by her. There were people in the church whom she had looked up to, but none reached out to her. Her attempts to communicate with the church's leadership were ignored.

Whether intended or not, the message we received was painfully clear: we had become an embarrassment. We had become a burden and a liability to the church, and it was best for everyone if we simply went away.

So we did. We left.

But it hurt. It hurt like hell.

Hitting Rock Bottom

The months after being cut loose and set adrift were very difficult times. I was still on medication and dealing with my depression. The excessive drinking continued at the same time.

My wife and I were also going through counselling. Our lives were so fractured that we were not even ready to see a counsellor together; we each saw a different therapist on our own. Neither one of us had any confidence that we could save our marriage.

During that season, I felt alone and hopeless.

More than anything, I wanted to die.

I remember thinking: "I have become such a problem for everyone. Why don't I do everyone a favour and just end it?"

Nothing mattered anymore. Not my work, not my life, and not my faith. In fact, the whole notion of God felt like a cruel joke.

Chapter Three: Dark Night Of The Soul

In some of my drunken moments late at night, I would, for some reason, remember the sermons that I used to preach – sermons on the faithfulness of God, on the church being a community of grace – and my own words mocked me. The only thing that was real to me was this all-consuming, ever-present darkness and loneliness.

During those times, I thought of Psalm 88:18, which described my life down to a tee: I had "no more friends or neighbours, and darkness was my closest friend."

It was my only reality.

Unexpected Hope

It is easy to make blanket statements like "The church does not show grace" simply based on the words and actions of some.

However, we must not forget that there are plenty of people in the church who are grace-giving, who practice love and forgiveness, and embrace those who are wounded.

Sometimes you may be surprised by who they are.

I know I was.

In my lowest moments, God used the most unexpected people to breathe hope into my life again. He chose to use the most unexpected ones to begin the work of re-creation.

One of them was my own daughter, who was three years old at the time. Taylor was an orphan whom we had adopted from China when she was just a baby.

Abandoned the day she was born and left to die on the streets on a cold winter day, a policeman found her and took her to an orphanage. It was a miracle she survived.

One night, I distinctly remember going into Taylor's room to check on her. Each time she sensed I was sitting on her bed next to her, she would reach for my arm and pull it tightly against her tiny chest. It was as if she was saying to me, "Don't go. Don't leave me. Don't let me be abandoned again."

It was during those quiet late-night moments in her room, when I looked at her while she slept, that a sense of purpose and hope began to stir in me again.

I whispered to her: "We both know what it feels like to be abandoned and left for dead. If you promise not to let go, I won't let go either, and we will figure this out together."

Unexpected Friends

God also used another unexpected group of people to come to our rescue. My wife and I had been mentoring a group of young adults ever since they were university students.

For over a decade, they regularly hung out in our home and shared meals with us over holiday seasons. In a way, we had almost become second parents to them.

When we left the church, it was this group of young people whom we were most worried about.

However, a few weeks after my resignation had been announced, one of them called and said: "We are coming over for dinner this Saturday," the same way they had done for years.

About 10 of them showed up. They brought food. They helped to set the table and brought out the extra folding chairs, as if nothing had changed.

Chapter Three: Dark Night Of The Soul

Then it was time for dinner to start.

For years, it had been customary for me to say grace at the beginning of our meals. To be honest, I was quietly dreading the thought of leading them in prayer. However, when the table was set and the food was ready, they simply started eating, without missing a beat in the conversation around the table.

They did not wait for me to say a prayer. There was no strained, awkward silence either.

> Even though I no longer held a "religious job", in their hearts and minds, nothing had changed.

It was clear that they had discussed it earlier and were determined to help me feel comfortable in their presence.

The message was loud and clear. Even though I no longer held a "religious job", in their hearts and minds, nothing had changed.

This same group of young people have continued to faithfully walk with us even though years have passed. They turned out to be the one group of people who had steadfastly refused to let us go. We continued to share many more dinners at our home, sharing both the good times and the bad times in our lives.

Through these years, we watched them get married, change jobs to pursue their dreams, relocate to other places in the world, and go through the ups and downs in life.

They never offered us counsel. They never even asked us what happened.

They simply stayed with us, walked with us and allowed us to continue to walk with them.

Nothing had changed.

The Real Ministry

Why was it that this group of young people could be there for us in our lowest moments and greatest time of need, while others couldn't – or *wouldn't*?

While everyone had his or her own reasons for their responses, I believe it boils down to our understanding of what "Christian ministry" is about. This group of young people understood something fundamental:

At its core, ministry is not "institutional." It is not merely about building, organizing or growing a church.

Neither is ministry "informational". It is not about having the right words to say, knowing the right verse for every situation or holding all the right doctrines.

Rather, what makes Christian ministry uniquely Christian – Christ-centred – is that it is *incarnational*. It is "Word becoming flesh and dwelling among us."

In the dark nights of my soul, when my heart and mind could not even entertain the idea of God, these friends became Jesus in the flesh to us. When we were weary and heavy-laden with unspeakable burdens during those days of terrible conflict and strife, they reached out, put their arms around us, and gave us rest.

Which brings me to the second question that still troubles me: will I ever be able to entrust myself to another community again?

Chapter Three: Dark Night Of The Soul

At this point, to be honest, I do not yet know.

While I commit my healing to God, my family is currently attending a new church right now. Our pastor is familiar with our story and has become a friend to me.

Occasionally on Sundays, whenever I listen to the message that is being preached, a part of me still feels so distant. I desperately want to believe what I am hearing. I want to "buy in". I want to be a part of what is going on.

But like a tuning fork that is somehow tuned to another frequency, my heart simply would not resonate with what I was hearing. My heart was telling me: "I don't belong here."

It is a very lonely feeling.

Let's Date A While
If I may offer a word to pastors… every Sunday when you stand up at the pulpit to preach, please remember that sitting in your pews are people like me.

We are hidden.

We have been hurt.

We do not know whether we can trust the church again.

Please be gentle and patient with us. We need time – but we do not know how long.

Please acknowledge that not everyone is ready to jump on board, and assure us that the train will wait for us; that it will not take off and leave us stranded on our own.

It will mean so much to us.

I would like to close this chapter with an excerpt from a book by author and pastor Michael Cheshire, *Why We Eat Our Own*. I read it while on a personal writing retreat.

Among The Ashes

In his book, he encouraged those of us who have been hurt and let down by the church to try going back. When I got to the portion below, I found my tears flowing freely:

For those of us who are still in local churches... while we understand your feelings about why you left, maybe for a moment you could hear the heart of those who stayed. Let us share with you how we feel about all this.
We miss you.
We miss the leadership you took with you.
We miss the wisdom you brought to the table.
We miss the gifts God gave you.
We miss your hands and feet that worked tirelessly to help others.
We miss your ability to question our bad habits.
We miss your smiles.
We miss being a family...
You know in your heart that we can do so much more good together than apart.
We don't have to get married.
Let's date a while. Come see if it's a good fit.
If some churches are unwilling to change and to grow in love and serving others, then avoid those.
But churches are still full of people who think, feel and believe just like you.
We have been standing on the walls and keeping the torches burning for better days ahead.
Many have been fighting for your place here.

Chapter Three: Dark Night Of The Soul

We can be a city on a hill again.
We can be hope to a fallen world.
We can use our resources, time and energy to do more than remodel the church offices every other year.
Let's meet tornadoes, floods, hurricanes and fires with waves of support, care, love, and money.
Let's do it better than anyone on earth.
Let's show up as a fully functioning army for the battle for the hearts of people; armed with love, forgiveness, grace, strength and humility.
Yeah, let's try this all again.
Let's get involved in more social issues.
Let's be friends again.
Let's be broken together, because broken people have the ability to heal each other in ways the unbroken can never understand.

– MICHAEL CHESIRE. *WHY WE EAT OUR OWN*.
FIRST PUNCH PRESS. KINDLE EDITION.

* * * * * *

Some day, perhaps, I might return.

Some day, I hope.

CHAPTER FOUR

"Look, I Make All Things New!"

> *"I know what I'm doing. I have it all planned out – plans to take care of you, not abandon you, plans to give you the future you hope for."*
>
> – Jeremiah 29:11, *The Message*

The other day, a good friend remarked to me: "You know, Alfred, your life is a miracle."

At first I did not quite know what she meant. There was no miraculous healing. No one was raised from the dead. I did not win the lottery. (OK, so my older daughter cleaned up her room voluntarily last week, so I guess that counts as a miracle of sorts!)

Seriously, we were just a regular family trying our best to cope with the highs and lows of life one day at a time. There was nothing special or miraculous there.

However, as I reflected on my friend's comment later that night, I recognized the truth in what she said.

Her statement reminded me of what C. S. Lewis once pointed out: "Miracles are a retelling in small letters of the very same story which is written across the whole world in letters too large for some of us to see."

In other words, the miracles that God performs in our lives are akin to the way a pastor uses illustrations in his sermons. When a preacher wants to explain an idea that may be too complex for our minds to grasp, he might draw an example from our everyday life – something we can relate to – in order to help us understand better.

An Intentional Life Story
It is now clear to me that God was actively writing my story even during the darkest days. More than anything else, this is my source of hope – the knowledge that my life moving forward is not simply a collection of random circumstances and happenings, but rather, it is a *planned narrative* with a caring Author, who is crafting every word, every page with care and purpose – even during the days when I had no idea if the sun would rise for me tomorrow.

That does not mean life will simply be one fairytale after another. Just because God is intentionally writing my story does not guarantee that I will never again experience health problems, marital issues, financial struggles or battle depression – or any other challenges that life throws at us.

However, when my friend observed that my life is a miracle, I realize that the "miracle" she was referring to was not simply about God supernaturally solving all my problems and healing my diseases. Rather, they are God's way of showing me that *the work He is doing in my life is the same work He is doing across creation.*

Chapter Four: "Look, I Make All Things New!"

My story – the one that He is still in the process of completing – is part of the *bigger story* that He has been writing since the beginning of time.

My hope is not built on some fairytale notion of "happily ever after". Rather, I have hope, because I know my life is part of the *bigger story* that points to the renewal of all creation, the promise of an ultimate new heaven and a new earth.

My life from day to day is a part of that new creation!

An Intimate Relationship
When I revisit what God is doing in my life through this new lens, I see my life as a microcosm of what God is doing across the whole world, as C. S. Lewis had said. For me, a by-product of that learning process is that the Bible now feels more intimate.

For the first time in my life, I saw the Bible as a story, at least in part, *about God and me*. In Chapter 2, I wrote about dealing with fear and craving intimacy with God. If you recall where I had come from, you might better understand why this is a huge step forward for me.

In particular, some of the BIG theological ideas I had learned by rote in seminary years ago began to take on a very real personal meaning to me. Two of these concepts became reality for me as I experienced them personally during this journey of renewal and rebirth:

- God's Work of Provision
- God's Work of Renewal

▪ GOD'S WORK OF PROVISION

In Genesis 3, the story is told of Adam and Eve's sin. Right away, God knew the magnitude of what had happened and the catastrophic implications for all of creation. Yet, while He had the salvation of the universe in mind, one little verse reveals how God cares even about the tiniest details of our lives: "The LORD God made garments of skin for Adam and his wife and *clothed them*" (Genesis 3:28, emphasis mine).

I have always found this verse strangely comforting. While the entire universe was reeling from the devastation of sin, God was still concerned with the practical needs of His children.

In my own life, it always amazed me to see how God had always provided for my family and I, especially during those very difficult years.

After I had resigned from the church, I had no idea how I would make a living. The church had granted me a severance package, but I knew that the money would eventually run out.

The reality was that I had lost my source of income and I did not know where the next dollar was going to come from.

Job Hunting

After about four months of sending out countless resumes and knocking on many doors, I managed to find a job within the field of community services. I had applied to be the executive director of a small agency that recruited

Chapter Four: "Look, I Make All Things New!"

volunteers for non-profit organizations and promoted volunteerism in the community.

The fact that I landed the job was a miracle in itself. Until then, I had had no experience in social services. I was honestly shocked when I received the phone call informing me that I had been chosen for the job.

I was almost tempted to ask, "Are you sure you have called the right person?"

Barely two weeks into the job, even before my new business cards were printed, I was greeted by one of the harsh realities of the sector.

I arrived at the office one morning and found a letter on my desk. It was from our primary funder. I opened the letter and it basically said that after reviewing their funding priorities, they had "made the difficult decision" to stop funding our agency.

A few days later, I received yet another letter from a different funder bearing the same bad news. Within a week, we had lost 90 percent of our funding! Our agency had less than 12 months to survive.

> It always amazed me to see how God had always provided for my family and I.

I looked at the small staff in our office and thought of their livelihood. I knew that I had to learn about the business in a BIG hurry in order to secure new funding and try to save their jobs. So I began meeting and speaking to anyone who was willing to talk to me.

I called people in the business, explained that I was a rookie and asked if I could have 20 minutes of their time to pick their brains. To my pleasant surprise, most of the people I approached were exceedingly kind and generous with their time.

Over the course of the next year, I drove thousands of kilometres, drank gallons of cold coffee in the car and met with hundreds of people across the social services landscape.

While I managed to secure some new funding in the end, the real benefit was the opportunity to learn from all these people. Little did I know it at the time, but that same knowledge base and network paved the way to my next job, which came along in a way that was every bit as "miraculous".

> That knowledge base and network paved the way to my next position.

I was driving home after work one afternoon, feeling discouraged because, despite all my fundraising efforts, it looked like our little agency would be forced to close down as our money was just about running out.

As I pulled into my driveway, my cell phone rang. It was a friend who had found out that I was working in the non-profit sector and wanted to tell me about another job opening. This time, it was not a position in a small agency, but a high-profile leadership role within a new, multi-million-dollar government-funded project.

Chapter Four: "Look, I Make All Things New!"

Just like my first job in the sector, I felt as though there was no way that I would qualify when I studied the job description. I knew enough to recognize that this was one of those "dream-job" opportunities that would attract many applications.

I thanked my friend for letting me know about the opportunity and sent in my resume with no expectations that I would be chosen for an interview, let alone actually getting the job.

> I was genuinely thankful for the opportunity, even if that was as far as I would go.

Surprisingly, I was selected for an interview. It was a wonderful experience to be interviewed by some of the top people in the business. I was genuinely thankful for the opportunity, even if that was as far as I would go.

Imagine my surprise when my phone rang again a week later. I was being offered the position!

My jaw was still on the floor even as I went through a flurry of training and orientation activities to prepare for my new job.

One afternoon as I was speaking to the trainer, she said to me, "Alfred, you will discover that the key to succeeding in this job is your ability to motivate people from wildly different backgrounds to pull together in the same direction, towards the same goal.

"You cannot think of this post as a position of power. You have to think of this as a position of servitude – your job is to lead in a way that supports and empowers others to succeed."

I remembered thinking to myself in amazement: *"That's exactly what I did for almost 20 years!"*

That was when I saw how the pieces fit together to make the miracle happen: God had a plan in the bigger scheme of things after all.

Nothing Wasted In God's Economy

Just when I thought the years spent in the ministry had been wasted, it turned out that God had been using those years to teach me how to become a leader and a servant at the same time.

Arguably, there is no better place on the planet than in the pastoral ministry where I could have learned how those two seemingly opposite qualities come together paradoxically to form this unique style of leadership – *exactly the kind of leadership my new position called for!*

Just when I thought that the few years of driving to hundreds of meetings with different people in the industry had been in vain because I had failed to save my agency, it turned out that those meetings had woven the network I needed for my next job.

Just when my agency was about to fold, my friend told me about the new job. Everything came together at just the right time, with the right people in all the right places!

I was reminded of Genesis 3:28 when God made the clothing and still took care of the man and woman – even when they had failed Him.

Chapter Four: "Look, I Make All Things New!"

I also thought of the passage in Jeremiah 29:11:

"I know what I'm doing. I have it all planned out – plans to take care of you, not abandon you, plans to give you the future you hope for."
(The Message)

For the first time in my life, I felt a truly intimate connection to those words – and to God Himself. He was not just the God who feeds the birds of the air and clothes the grass of the field. The God who made the clothing for Adam and Eve in the beginning of time, is the same God who "miraculously" provides for me today.

Like C. S. Lewis observed, "Miracles are a retelling in small letters of the very same story which is written across the whole world in letters too large for some of us to see."

• GOD'S WORK OF RENEWAL

If you ask most Christians what the Bible has to say about God's work of renewal, chances are, you will hear some theory about how God will come back one day, right all wrongs and make a new world.

Most Christians think of God's work of renewal for all creation as something that God does on His own, apart from us. In Sunday school, we are taught to look forward to the day when Jesus comes back and makes all things new. We are taught to watch and wait.

However, my own journey with depression and recovery from the devastation I had caused taught me something new: God's work of renewal – which ultimately extends to the entire creation – is, in fact, something that He is doing *through* us! We are not merely idle bystanders or passive spectators waiting for God to come back with a new heaven and a new earth. Rather, God is creating this new heaven and new earth by creating... *a new me!*

Here is a fascinating thought to consider:

What if we are called to play a much more active role than simply "watch and wait"?

What if God's "new world" is, in fact, a mosaic that comprises all the "new worlds" that He is creating in each of our lives?

Turning A New Page
Today, as I reflect on my family's journey, I am amazed at how we have changed, compared to just a few years ago.

Anna and I have truly turned a new page. Our marriage, our philosophies toward parenthood, the priorities that we live by, our theology and approach to faith… have all been *made new*.

Today, we find ourselves living life deeper and being more honest than ever before. Unlike the years when we were in full-time church ministry, the overarching question "what will others think?" no longer governs our actions or registers as a concern for us.

Today, we are much more honest with our emotions and the realities that are part of living with depression.

We know there are good days and bad days.

We manage each day as best as we can.

Chapter Four: "Look, I Make All Things New!"

We are learning to see each day for what it is: another page in the story of renewal that God is writing across the universe – not just for us, but for all of creation.

We see ourselves as characters in this grand story, following the plot which uses our lives to create a better world – right where we are each day.

> God is creating this new heaven and new earth by creating... *a new me!*

It may involve encouraging a friend who is struggling.

It may mean sharing kindness with someone at work who is going through a tough time.

It may mean raising our kids to dream ridiculously big dreams in order to change the world.

Through it all, we are convinced of one thing: God is not only doing His work of renewal *in* us, but He is also doing the same work *through* us.

This hit home one day when I was giving a speech to a group of new immigrants as part of my work. I tried my best to encourage them as they began their new journeys in a new country.

Afterwards, a Spanish-speaking woman came forward to speak to me. In her broken English, she asked if I was a Christian. I was not sure why she asked, but I said yes.

She smiled and said, "I knew it. I can see Jesus in you when you spoke."

That was all she wanted to tell me.

With that, she turned and left.

* * * * * *

I thought back to that despondent day years ago when I sat all alone in McDonalds that first Christmas Sunday after I had left the church, staring forlornly into my coffee cup.

Then I thought about where we are today as a family. And the words of my friend rang clearly in my mind:

My life is a miracle.

It is the same miracle that God is performing day by day as He weaves our stories together into His Great Story of renewal for all creation.

Or, in Jesus' words of hope from my favourite scene in *Passion Of The Christ*: "Look, I make all things new!"

Your Life Matters

I feel that it is important to tell my story because I know firsthand how hope often becomes the first casualty that is lost in one's battle with depression.

I also know for those struggling in the darkness of depression, hopelessness is not in believing that our lives will never get better; rather, it is the belief that our lives no longer matter.

That is why I wanted to write this book. If there is only one thing that you take away, please believe this: your life *does* matter.

Your life matters because it is an irreplaceable part of God's story of renewal. It is not the same without *you*. You are the ONE whom He pursues, leaving the other 99 who are already safe.

Chapter Four: "Look, I Make All Things New!"

You may not be able to see it now, but God is writing a new page. He has not stopped writing your story, just as He did not stop writing mine even through the darkest days. God is doing a new work in you and through you; *He is making all things new.*

The Scriptures remind us in 2 Corinthians 4:16-18:

"Therefore we do not lose heart.

*Though outwardly we are wasting away,
yet inwardly we are being renewed day by day.*

*For our light and momentary troubles
are achieving for us an eternal glory
that far outweighs them all.*

*So we fix our eyes not on what is seen,
but on what is unseen, since what is seen is
temporary, but what is unseen is eternal."*

Daily Miracles

By the way, when I say that what happened to us was a miracle, I certainly do not want to create an impression that everything happened supernaturally, at the snap of a finger. The truth is, there was a lot of gut-wrenching hard work involved.

When Anna and I decided to remain committed to each other after my affair, we were determined to not only "stay married", but to rebuild our marriage from scratch.

With that, we began intensive counselling that lasted for five years. We left no stones unturned in discovering the reasons why our marriage had failed in the first place. The process was excruciatingly painful at times. But we are convinced now that the work was worth it.

We will be celebrating our 22nd wedding anniversary in 2014. Our marriage is a daily miracle that we could not have imagined when our lives caved in a few years ago.

New Chapters

In the last chapter, I wrote about our daughter Taylor who was an orphan whom we had adopted from China.

Today, Taylor has grown into a vibrant, beautiful 10-year-old girl. She is so full of life and everyone who meets her instantly falls in love with her.

I remember watching Taylor play hockey early one Saturday morning. As I sat in the stands watching her handle the hockey stick like a real pro, I thought to myself, for a baby abandoned on the streets of China on the day of her birth, what are the odds of her playing ice hockey in this country called Canada a decade later?

> The process was excruciatingly painful at times... but the work was worth it.

That is why, whenever I hear people say, "Miracles just don't happen anymore", I always smile on the inside and say to them, "You need to meet Taylor!"

Oh, and just as Anna, Taylor and I were settling into this new stage of our lives as a family, we received yet

Chapter Four: "Look, I Make All Things New!"

another huge surprise, another miracle. Out of the blue, Anna said three words to me that I thought I'd never hear:

"I am pregnant!"

On 12 June 2012, at 2:33am, Anna gave birth to our second daughter, Mackenzie Jaclyn Sam Yuet Lam, whom we now affectionately call MJ.

After 20 years of marriage, when we least expected it, God turned a new page in our story and started writing a new plot – one that we could never have imagined in our wildest dreams.

I am reminded of His promise and how it has come to pass: "Look, I make all things new!"

CHAPTER FIVE

A Radical "What If" Community

"And I pray that you, being rooted and established in love, may have power, together with all the Lord's holy people, to grasp how wide and long and high and deep is the love of Christ."

– Ephesians 3:17-18

Have you ever had an unexpected encounter that would change your life forever? I have. In 2003, I had accepted a six-month teaching contract in Asia. One weekend, Anna and I took a three-day vacation to Bangkok, Thailand.

Underneath its booming tourism industry, Bangkok has some of the most extreme poverty that I have ever seen in a "modern city". No matter which way we turned, there seemed to be endless lines of people on the streets, their hands outstretched, begging for a living.

They came in all shapes and sizes – from older folks and people with visible disabilities to entire families, with children as young as three or four years old.

I did not know what was more disturbing to me – this sea of humanity living in extreme poverty, or how quickly I became "desensitized" to the sight of human suffering only after a few days.

One afternoon, Anna and I were returning to our hotel after doing some shopping. On our way back, we passed by the usual crowds of beggars along the streets. As we made the last turn towards our hotel, I made eye contact with a beggar who would end up changing my life forever.

* * * * * *

In one way, this beggar was no different from the hundreds of others we have seen. His clothes were soiled and worn. He smelled like he had probably not had a bath in days. I was about to walk by when he suddenly looked at me.

It was then that I noticed something different about him: *he had no arms!* He kneeled on the street, holding a paper cup between his teeth, and spent most of his days staring down at the ground. I do not know what made him look up at the precise moment I passed by, but when our eyes met, something in his searching eyes made me stop.

I tried to reach into my pockets to give him some loose change. But my arms were so full with our shopping bags that I was having trouble freeing up my hands.

After struggling to balance my load, I managed to drop a couple of coins into his cup.

Even as I walked away, my mind kept replaying the scene over and over again.

Chapter Five: A Radical "What If" Community

It almost seemed like a modern-day parable – a story about two strangers, both created by God, meeting on the poverty-stricken streets of Bangkok.

One had no arms and had to hold a cup between his teeth just to beg for a living.

The other, a minister and a seminary professor, had his arms so loaded with shopping bags that he could not free up a hand to help.

What is wrong with this picture?

Later that evening, Anna and I went for a stroll after supper. We sat on the front steps of a beautiful hotel to enjoy the "breeze" of air-conditioning from the lobby.

Ironically, while we looked on the streets lined with poverty, a live band was playing inside the hotel. I listened closer and recognized the song "What A Wonderful World" by Louis Armstrong.

As I took in the scene of human suffering before me, the irony was striking. While poverty was rampant out on the streets, there was

> **In that terrible juxtaposition, I saw a damning satire of North American Christianity.**

"What A Wonderful World" playing inside.

While I felt the scorching heat on my face as we sat on those steps, my back was cooled by the comfortable air-conditioned breeze.

In that terrible juxtaposition, I saw a damning satire of North American Christianity, something in which I have been a part of throughout my entire adult life. Every week, Sunday after Sunday, we gather to worship God in plush and beautiful multi-million-dollar church buildings that feature the latest audio-visual technology.

Yet, while we enjoy our "wonderful world" inside, outside of our "bubble" is a world that is suffering and dying, in every way imaginable.

The "Good News"

In the sci-fi movie *2012*, the story is told of a world faced with a cataclysmic super disaster that threatened a global tsunami which would wipe out the entire planet. With time running out, the leaders of the G8 gathered to come up with a plan to ensure the survival of the human species.

> While we enjoy our "wonderful world" inside, outside is a world that is dying.

Enormous arks were built with the latest technology to save enough people to survive the end of the world and rebuild human civilization afterwards.

Only 400,000 people were chosen to board the arks. This meant that only the "chosen elite" of the human race were selected, including top scientists, doctors, teachers, artists, the educated and the skilled.

The plot followed how the main characters struggled to get into the arks before the end arrived and be included among those who were "saved".

Chapter Five: A Radical "What If" Community

The storyline is a perfect description of our present understanding of the Christian faith, or more precisely, what we call the "Good News".

That is, this world as we know it is heading towards ultimate destruction and we must find a way to save it.

The "Good News" is that God has provided a way for a relative few to survive the destruction of the "old world" and spend eternity with Him in the "new world". The entire human race is separated into two camps: "In" or "Out", "Saved" or "Unsaved".

> The entire human race is separated into two camps: "In" or "Out", "Saved" or "Unsaved".

A quick glance at a typical Christian church on any Sunday morning may convince some that the selection criteria for who is to be "saved" is the same as that in the movie *2012* – only the "elite" gets chosen.

Somewhere along the line, we also bought into the public image of "the successful church" as one that has huge, impressive buildings, well-dressed staff, comfortable sanctuaries, professionally run facilities, slick and well choreographed worship services, to name a few.

There have been plenty of unfortunate (and unjustified) criticisms of large churches being "self-serving" just because they spent money on buildings and facilities.

While it is not necessary nor helpful to cast judgment on those large churches with beautiful facilities or debate whether it is a "right" or "wrong" way to spend their resources, churches – like individuals – spend the most money on what they think is most important.

The typical evangelical church's approach of spending vast sums of money on facilities is driven by a philosophy or theology that says that the most important thing for the church to do is to get people into the "saved" category. The way that it happens is for people to hear and analyze a presentation of the evidence for Christianity – and then make a logical, conscious decision to "accept Christ". Therefore, we feel it is our prime responsibility to put people in the most comfortable surroundings possible to encourage them to "sign up", thus the huge investments on buildings and facilities.

> The typical evangelical church's approach... is to get people into the "saved" category.

Sadly, according to those "entrance requirements", people like the beggar I met in Bangkok will not be "in".

He might have lived in poverty and suffering his whole life.

He might have lost his arms through a tragic accident.

He might never have known – even for a second in his life – what it is like to be held and loved. There could have been a thousand tragic twists and turns in his life story.

He may not even have the intellectual abilities to understand our "gospel presentation".

Chapter Five: A Radical "What If" Community

According to the "version of Christianity" that I used to believe in, that brand of theology says none of that matters because when that beggar arrives at the "Final Judgment", the only question God will care about is whether he had made "the right choice" in order to be included among the ones who were "saved".

If he had not, God would send him to the eternal damnation of hell.

Is this really "Good News" for him?

A Radical New Way

I wonder if we might have thought about God's grace and salvation the wrong way. Here is something to consider:

What if the "Good News" that Jesus came to preach is much wider, higher and deeper than that?

What if, rather than selecting only a few to escape the ultimate destruction of the world, God is calling all of us to work together with Him to repair the damage caused by sin and help create a new world together?

What if, instead of drawing another "line in the sand" to divide the human race into two camps, the gospel is about God *erasing every single line* that has ever been drawn to separate people from each other and from Him?

Some of those lines etched on the pages of human history are so deep, so long, so wide, so dark that nothing

> Have we thought about God's grace and salvation the wrong way?

could erase them. So God used the blood of His own Son to once and for all paint over them.

Paul tells us in Galatians 3:28: "There is neither Jew nor Greek, there is neither slave nor free, there is no male and female, for you are all one in Christ Jesus."

The three divisions that Paul mentioned represented the most historically established, culturally accepted, iron-clad, etched-in-stone categories that separated people.

> There was absolutely no possible way for anyone to cross the divide.

Those lines – racial/religious ("neither Jew nor Greek); socio-economic ("neither slave nor free"); and sex/gender ("no male or female") are drawn so deep, the chasms so wide, the walls so high, that they have separated and categorized the entire human race without exception to one camp or the other.

There was absolutely no possible way for anyone to cross the divide.

But here is the Good News, according to Paul:

God's love expressed in Christ Jesus reaches deeper, farther, higher, wider than all of those means of separation, and has brought the entire human race together to Himself.

That redemptive message was so radical, so explosive, – beyond imagination or comprehension – that it would have sounded absolutely scandalous or even blasphemous to those who originally heard them from the lips of Paul.

Chapter Five: A Radical "What If" Community

To appreciate the impact of those words, here is an example of how they might sound to today's church:

There is now neither churched nor unchurched, religious nor secular, Christian nor Muslim, gay nor straight, male nor female nor transgendered, for you are all one in Christ Jesus.

Did you find those words unsettling? Did they cause you to shift uncomfortably as you read them? Deep within our fallen human nature, we find safety in boundaries, lines, structures and categories. We find our security,
in part, in knowing where we "fit".

Yet that is precisely the good news that Jesus brought: "The only thing that matters is for you to know that you belong to Me. You fit with Me. *Regardless of who you are.*"

All Sinners Saved By Grace

Whether you are a banker from Wall Street, a Catholic priest from Rome or a beggar from the slums in Bangkok, they all share exactly the same standing before God.

As far as He is concerned, each one of them has been painstakingly created, stubbornly sought after, sacrificially redeemed, unconditionally forgiven and forever loved.

What will the church look like if we really believe that?

What if the church becomes a place where we belong not because of which religion we have chosen or what creed we have signed on, but simply because of what Jesus has done for us?

What if the church is not a place where we simply congratulate ourselves for being different from the rest of the "outside world", but the one place in the world where we truly are all the same?

What will a community like that look like?

When I spoke with people in the church who felt they must keep their struggle with mental illness a secret rather than seeking help from their community, can you guess what was the number one reason they mentioned?

The reply is always the same:

"I don't want people to treat me differently."

As one who has struggled with depression too, I longed for a real community that would not treat me "differently". I did not want to automatically be allocated into a "special support group". I simply wanted a place to belong, to be a part of a community – just like anyone else.

> I simply wanted a place to belong, to be a part of a community – just like anyone else.

Virtually every voice in the mental health sector echoes the importance of community. Beyond medication, treatment and counselling, community is always cited as the key factor in the recovery and healing process for someone with a mental illness.

If community is the "game changer", shouldn't the church be better at this than anyone else? The puzzling thing is, why do so many churches claim that they are

Chapter Five: A Radical "What If" Community

"not equipped" to "deal with" someone who has a mental health issue?

Perhaps when we, as a church, claim we are not ready nor equipped to "deal with" someone with a mental illness, what we really mean is that, doing so will inconvenience us or "get in the way" of our efforts to reach or minister to "normal" people.

Not those we do not understand.
Not those who are "beneath" us.
Not those who are too "different".

Those We Reject
While writing this chapter, a tremendous sadness hit me as it occurred to me that people who feel most excluded by the church today are precisely the kind of people whom Jesus went to great lengths to find, embrace, and include in His Kingdom: the homeless, those who have sinned and failed, those who are divorced, people who struggle with mental illnesses, those who have been cast aside and forgotten by our society, like that beggar I met in Bangkok.

Ironically, I cannot think of any other person who has impacted my life so powerfully.

That one moment in time back in 2003 when I locked eyes with that beggar in Bangkok changed my life forever.

Subconsciously, over the past 10 years, my "Christian worldview" has been developed in a large part through the lens of that beggar's eyes.

In a way, you can say that he has had tremendous "Christian influence" in my life.

Yet, the tragedy is, I doubt that he would be welcomed by most of our churches today, should he show up.

Which is sad, because as I look back on that moment on the streets of Bangkok, more and more I have begun to wonder… if that was the first time that I might have truly encountered Jesus.

CHAPTER SIX

We Can Do Better

*"Neither do people pour new wine into old wineskins.
If they do, the skins will burst;
the wine will run out and the wineskins will be ruined.*

*No, they pour new wine into new wineskins,
and both are preserved."*

– MATTHEW 9:17

Living with depression has been my daily reality for over 10 years. Some days, the urge to quit is strong, and the temptation to end it all is ever so appealing. It is a daily "invisible" battle that wounds the heart and scars the soul.

About a year after resigning as a pastor, I had the opportunity to volunteer with the Speakers' Bureau of the Canadian Mental Health Association (York Region).

We were a group of individuals from all walks of life who had been diagnosed with various forms of mental illnesses. Our stories were all different, but we shared a common desire to raise awareness and reduce stigma for mental health.

Often, we were invited to speak at college classes, corporate meetings and different community events.

When it was my turn, I always spoke about depression in the present tense, emphasizing the point that it is not something that I have "conquered", but it is very much a part of my everyday journey – quite likely for the rest of my days on earth.

I wanted my audience to grasp the fact that I was not addressing them as an "expert" on the subject, but rather, a mere fellow traveller. To my surprise, what often resonates most with the audience is the very fact that I have *not* overcome depression, that it is an ongoing battle which I have learned to fight and conquer one day at a time.

I have also learned that it is our struggles, rather than our victories, that truly encourage others on their journeys.

* * * * * *

In his book, *The Purpose Driven Life*, Pastor Rick Warren wrote: "Other people are going to find healing in your wounds. Your greatest life messages and your most effective ministry will come out of your deepest hurts."

I have been thinking about that a lot lately as I am writing this book.

Chapter Six: We Can Do Better

I used to think that people were drawn to stories of struggles and pain because, as the old adage says, "Misery loves company."

However, my own experience with depression has taught me something else. I now understand that people are not necessarily attracted to stories of pain as much as they are drawn to the *people* behind the stories – those who understand pain.

> **People are... drawn to the *people* behind the stories, people who understand pain.**

I remembered sitting down with the other volunteers on the Speakers' Bureau when I first joined them. In addition to sharing a common passion to help others, I discovered that each of us bore scars from our own battles. Some had lost long careers that they enjoyed.

One person said to me: "As much as I am enjoying what I am doing now, I miss what I did before. I miss it all the time – every day."

Others shared their lifelong pain of loneliness:

"We live in a culture that celebrates strength and shuns weakness. I was afraid that if I showed weakness by telling others about my struggles, I too, would be shunned."

Stigmatizing The Suffering

Pain and suffering invariably changes a person. In my journey, I have discovered that our hurts and our pain are unique instruments that God uses to refine us, making us into better people.

Listening to various personal stories from our group, I could not help but notice how absolutely "upside down" our society can be. Sadly, the media has created an image of mental health patients as being prone to violence.

Yet the reality is the exact opposite: those living with mental illness are far more likely to be *victims* – rather than perpetrators – of violence.

There is so much stigma about those suffering from mental illness. They are branded as being "emotionally weak", but the truth is, the people whom I have gotten to know in the group are truly among some of the strongest I have met.

> "My mental illness has truly been a gift... albeit wrapped in barbed wire!"

What impressed me the most was not only their bravery in speaking out, but their courage to stand against the tide of culture and redefine how life is supposed to "work".

One person says: "People say I have a 'disorder', but as I battle my way through life, with a purpose and passion to help others along the way, I feel that my life has never been more *'in order'*!"

"My mental illness has truly been a gift… albeit wrapped in barbed wire!" chuckles another. "It has given me the desire to connect with people and share my story, not to hand out answers, but to share hope. And THAT is the singular most important thing for all of us."

Our wounds strengthen us. Our pain changes us.

If other people are going to find healing in our wounds, as Rick Warren points out, then should not the church take special care in how we treat the wounded?

Not only because that is our duty, but also because they are living "treasures" that enrich our community and enhance our ministry.

Unfortunately, we often end up doing the opposite.

Loving (Not Labelling) The Wounded
Since leaving the church, I have had conversations with a few pastors who had left the ministry for various reasons. One common thread that runs through those conversations is the hurt they felt when people started treating them as if they had become strangers.

That is something I can personally relate to. When the news of my resignation got out, almost overnight, people started treating me differently. They would either pretend not to see me, or if they did, they literally "looked" at me differently. I could feel the condemnation in their eyes.

Once we have put a label on people, the labels are all we see:

"She is divorced."
"He has mental issues."
"He had an affair."
"They support gay-marriage."
"She is pro-choice."

We stop seeing people as people. We simply look at the labels we put on them, and treat them as if they are the sum of their ideas, beliefs, disease or sin.

Perhaps some of you who are reading these words have known pastors or ministers who have gone through similar circumstances. Your leaders might have left the ministry because they had made mistakes.

When you found out, you might have been disappointed or very angry. You may have wanted to demand some sort of public acknowledgement or confession.

You may have had your own ideas about how they should have been disciplined or punished. You might even have felt that they should have been asked to leave the church and never be allowed back into ministry again.

> We stop seeing people as people. We simply look at the labels we put on them...

Your feelings of hurt, disappointment, anger and betrayal are all reasonable and understandable. I have no intention to deny or minimize them in any way.

Rather, I simply want to point out one thing for your consideration: that pastor whom today you discovered had "fallen" or "stumbled" is the same person yesterday who, for years, had selflessly given himself to serve the church.

Chances are, he is the same person who tirelessly and faithfully visited the sick, cared for the elderly, counselled those who were struggling.

Chapter Six: We Can Do Better

He is the same person who stayed up late into the night week after week, trying his best to put together a sermon that would help the congregation.

Yes, so he had sinned. So he made a mistake. But that does not negate who he is and everything he has lived for.

Can we, for a moment, resist the temptation to slap a label on him and then simply discard him like damaged goods?

Can we, for a moment, consider the fact that there is a story, a context behind what had happened, and that a lot of pain might have been involved?

> Can we consider the fact that there is a story, a context behind what had happened?

Can we try to see him as a wounded brother in need of help rather than just a perpetrator of a terrible sin?

Can we consider the possibility that, after ministering to the church all these years, the pastor needs the church to minister to him for once, rather than judge and reject him?

If we call ourselves a community of grace, should it not be at times like this when, all the more, grace should shine through?

That Contagious Thing Called Grace

One thing I have learned about grace is that it is highly contagious. One evident tell-tale sign that someone has "contracted" or received grace is that he becomes gracious and grace-giving himself.

He cannot help it. He gives grace to the next person – and the next person gives grace to the next, and that is how grace works to change the world.

Besides being contagious, it is also highly addictive. Once you have tasted grace, you cannot help but go back for more.

Can you imagine how our churches will be influenced and shaped if we have honest pastors who have personally experienced the grace of forgiveness through failure?

Can you picture the richness of the ministries of those pastors who – after an appropriate season of healing and restoration – are welcomed, even encouraged, to return to serve in the church?

> Once you have tasted grace, you cannot help but go back for more.

Can you imagine what happens in those churches where grace is not only preached, but experienced and lived out by the one doing the preaching?

We deliver sermon after sermon on the lives of Bible heroes like Jacob, Moses, David, Samson, Peter and Paul. We so eloquently proclaim God to be a "God of second chances" who uses the lives of those who have failed to accomplish great things for him.

In my own experience, I have seen very few examples of that in our churches. Too often, people who have failed leave their ministries, their churches, their communities – and never come back.

As a young pastor who was only just starting out in the ministry at the time, I remember a veteran pastor warning me: "Ministry is the most unforgiving profession there is."

It was not until recently that I fully appreciated the irony of those words.

Please do not misunderstand me. I am not writing this to try and plead my own case. I am not trying to excuse or trivialize the seriousness of sin.

Of all people, having been the cause of much angst in my congregation, I understand full well the far-reaching and destructive consequences of a moral stumble. I am not denying the church has a responsibility to discipline and restore those who have sinned.

I am simply saying that as a community of grace, *we can do better*.

A Grace-centred community is fiercely protective of the wounded. It provides a safe environment, without judgment or condemnation, rumours and gossip. It is a haven where the important work of correction, healing, restoration and renewal can take place.

A Grace-centred community relentlessly pursues those who have been hurt. Rather than simply allowing them to walk away and disappear, it calls out to them, saying: "Our doors remain open for you."

It runs after them. It chases them down.

It knocks on their doors and says, "Please come back."

A Grace-centred community is steadfast in hope. It is not satisfied to have simply "followed the procedure" and "handled the situation". It refuses to let go of the hope of seeing the person restored. Instead, it seeks the renewal of the entire community as God redeems the brokenness created by sin.

Can you see how a community like that cannot help but be "contagious" and "addictive"?

That Liberating Thing Called Forgiveness
In the last 10 years, battling daily with depression has been a shattering journey.

At times, it felt as though every aspect of my life was crumbling to pieces – my work, my health, my friendships, my marriage and my family.

When I examined my life, there was not a single facet about which I could truly say, "There, I am solid *there*."

Yet, going through some of the darkest valleys of my life has transformed me into a new person.

> Going through some of the darkest valleys of my life has transformed me into a new person.

Now I understand that it was all part of the *essential process* of dismantling every part of my life, so it could be rebuilt from the ground up.

God did not make all things new in my life through some sort of deep intellectual awakening or supernatural spiritual experiences. Rather, He transformed me using the same two instruments He has made available to us: grace and forgiveness.

Chapter Six: We Can Do Better

Grace and forgiveness became my instruments of freedom. They freed me from destructive ideas that had imprisoned me for practically my entire life:

"You must be strong."

"You cannot show weakness."

"If you fail, no one will love you anymore."

When grace and forgiveness were extended to me by my friends and family – and most importantly, my wife – it taught me to begin doing something that I had never learned how to do, despite my having preached about those concepts for years: extending grace and forgiveness to myself.

> **God has forgiven you.**
> **We have forgiven you.**
> **But you need to** *forgive yourself.*

For people who have failed, especially those who have held leadership positions, that is often the most difficult thing to do.

We want to make restitution for our wrongs.

We want to pay for our mistakes.

We want to "fall on our swords" and endure the "punishment" that is befitting our transgression.

But we do not know how to forgive ourselves.

Yet that is such a crucial step in the process towards being made new. For a community that is learning to be better, perhaps the first step is in wrapping its arms around their wounded and saying to them, "God has forgiven you. We have forgiven you. But you need to *forgive yourself*."

Healed Vessels

In the end, that is the good news I want to share through this book: *God is doing something new.* He is creating new life in us, in the midst of our deepest pain, even when all seems dark and hopeless.

In Matthew 9:17, we are told about new wine and new wineskins. Jesus used the imagery to illustrate the work that He was doing by ushering in a new era and a new understanding of what God is trying to do in the world.

He compares that to a "new wine" that the traditional religious structures (the "old wineskin") cannot accept.

Like the image of the new wine that the Bible talks about in Matthew 9:17, this new life is actively fermenting. It is breathing…
it is expanding…
it is growing…
it is in the process of *getting better*.

> God wants the church to be the kind of new wineskin that will protect the new wine…

We do not yet know the full beauty of the wine that will be produced in the end. But in the incubating process, this new wine is too active and too explosive to be contained by the same old wineskins. The wineskin has to change.

In the same way, God wants to create new wineskins – and new communities – that will incubate and nurture the renewal process.

I believe that God wants the church to be the kind of new wineskin that will protect the new wine without suffocating it, and guide the fermentation process without constricting it.

Just as God works to change the lives of individuals, He is also at work to change churches, creating new wine and new wineskin at the same time.

Can all of us become new again? God believes we can – He has always had a vision for His church to be a healing vessel for sinners and the wounded.

If God believes that we can be healed and that we can be better, then we *can* – and we must.

Epilogue

*"I have fought the good fight,
I have finished the race,
I have kept the faith."*

– 2 Timothy 4:7

An old Chinese saying goes like this: "As one travels a thousand miles to present a feather as a gift, the gift is light, but the heart behind it is weighty."

That is exactly how I feel about this book.

When I set out to write this book, I did not intend to write the definitive word on the relationship between mental health and faith. This book is not meant to be a "heavyweight" on the subject. I only wanted to share my story, with the hope that it would encourage you.

An old seminary professor once gave me a sage word of advice: "Alfred, if you learn to communicate to hurting people, you will never lack an audience."

Some of you are reading this book in the midst of your own pain. You do not have time for page after page of idle words and worn-out clichés.

We may be different in every way imaginable, but pain is the one thing that unites us. I know I am not alone in the painful experiences that I have gone through, and I also know that just as God continues to do His work in me, He longs to do it in you too.

So please do not quit.

Do not stop fighting the good fight.

Do not stop running the race.

Do not stop believing.

Despite the darkness and brokenness, the tears will stop, the pain will cease, and most importantly, as God promised, *He will make all things new* – and that includes YOU.

* * * * * *

Writing this book proved to be more difficult than I had ever imagined. Besides the hard work of crafting thoughts into words – which every writer knows all too well – I was not quite prepared for how much it hurt to revisit some of my past experiences and memories.

> Just as God continues to do His work in me, He longs to do it in you too.

I remember very distinctly that fateful morning when I was about to announce my resignation from the church.

It was, without a doubt, the worst day of my life.

My wife Anna and I decided ahead of time that unlike our usual routine of going to church as a family, I would go to church alone that morning.

Epilogue

I woke up early, having been unable to sleep much the night before. I got dressed quietly, without exchanging a single word with Anna. In those days, words between us were few and far in between.

My young daughter was a little confused as to why I was the only one going to church. Sensing that something was not right, she kept quiet. The house was shrouded in a blanket of icy silence.

I remained in my room, trying to delay the inevitable. I took my time tying my tie as if it was the most important thing I had to do that day.

When it was finally time to leave, I went downstairs, where my wife and daughter were having breakfast.

As I walked past them on my way out, I did not say a word. My wife did not even look up.

I sat down on the staircase near the front door to put on my shoes. Just then, I heard the telephone ring. Anna came out shortly, handing me the phone.

"It's your dad," she said.

I picked up the phone.

Dad said, "How are you doing, son?"

Upon hearing his voice and the kindness in it, tears welled up in my eyes. It had been so long since I had heard a kind word from anyone.

I will never forget what he said to me next:

Among The Ashes

"Son, I want you to know that you will be OK. Life is not always smooth-sailing. Remember when I lost everything? I got back up, so can you."

* * * * * *

My father's words brought me back in time to when I was a young boy. When the Hong Kong stock market crashed in the 1970s, within one year the market had lost a whopping 90 percent of its value.

Like many others at that time, dad lost everything. During those dark days in Hong Kong, many people committed suicide. Some abandoned their families and simply ran away.

> "Remember when I lost everything? I got back up, so can you."

We had to move out of our comfortable apartment and into a small rented space. My dad had to work longer and longer hours at multiple jobs to make ends meet.

I recall one particular Mid-Autumn Festival. On the night of the festival, Chinese families traditionally spend time together, much like Thanksgiving in the West.

That day, my dad had to work late. So my mom bought a little paper lantern for my sister and I to play with.

As I ran around on our street, playing with the other kids in the neighbourhood, I happened to look over at my

Epilogue

mom who was sitting on the front steps watching us play. For some reason, she was crying. Tears were streaming down her face. I only found out later that she had spent the last few cents in her pocket that evening to buy that one paper lantern for my sister and I to share.

In terms of business success, life had not been kind to my dad. A few years after the stock market disaster of the mid 1970s, through hard work, he saved up enough money to start his own small business.

However, just when things started to look promising, the global recession in the early 1980s dealt my dad with another blow and the business ultimately failed. He would experience another setback in the 1990s that again took away all that he had.

> Through all of it, my dad steadfastly refused to quit.

I cannot recall many of the details from those earlier years way back then. I was too young to fully understand what was going on. All I knew was that they were difficult years for my parents.

However, the one thing that left an indelible mark in my memory as a young man was that, through it all, my dad steadfastly refused to quit. He never shirked any of his responsibilities to his family.

The simple words my dad said to me on the phone that final morning before I made my announcement at church might have sounded like fluff inside a greeting card to any random listener. But coming from my dad, they were rich words of personally-lived wisdom, solid enough for me to anchor on – at a time when everything else in my life was falling apart.

Leaving A Legacy
As parents, most of us spare no expense in our attempts to put our children on the right paths to success. Some spend tens of thousands of dollars on sports. Others hire the best music teachers or academic tutors for their children.

In Hong Kong where I was born, it is customary for parents to hire private tutors for their children, starting as young as Grade One. It is not uncommon for parents to camp outside popular kindergartens to try and get their kids enrolled so as to give them the best chance of getting a place in a well-known, prestigious "big name" school.

We all want our children to succeed. However, I have learned that the most valuable legacy that parents can leave their kids may lie in how they handle failure rather than in how much they prepare them for success.

> The most valuable legacy parents can leave their kids may lie in how they handle failure.

After speaking briefly with my father that morning, I was convicted again of why I had chosen to stand in front of my church to announce my resignation instead of simply running away.

Epilogue

Ultimately, it is the same reason why I decided to write this book: I want my failure to be documented so that, just like my dad did for me, my story of how I handled failure can become the legacy that I leave for my children.

Whatever meagre successes I have had or will experience are relatively inconsequential to the lives of my girls.

As they grow up, they will each pursue the paths of their choosing. Each will decide what success means to them. They will experience life differently than I have.

Wherever their lives take them, I want to be able to inspire my children by saying to them, just as my father encouraged me:

"Stay in the fight. Run the race. Keep the faith."

My children will have to fight their own fights, run their own races and own their own faith. Whichever way they go, one thing I know for certain is that there will be times when they will make mistakes.

They will fail.

They will stumble and fall.

When that happens, I want to be able to share with them the same life-tested words that my dad had for me:

"I got back up, so can you."

APPENDIX A

When Love Hurts
A Wife's Journey – By Anna Lam

Being married to a pastor – and being a pastor's wife – has its challenges. As a pastoral couple, we basically spent all our time in ministry. The church was literally our home and our entire life. That not only meant overseeing church events, but also included dealing with stressful situations and personal crises of church members.

However, something far more devastating than ministry challenges was about to turn our lives upside down.

When Depression Struck
At the time when the crisis occurred that caused our world to crash, Alfred had been in ministry for about 14 years and we had been married for 10 years.

Six years into our marriage, I noticed Alfred being "not happy". He often came home after ministry looking very tired and worn out. He also seemed very sad at times.

When I asked him how he was doing, his reply was: "I am fine, I'm just tired."

Being heavily involved in various church ministries as a pastoral couple, "being tired" was the norm. Naturally, I did not think much about it.

Until one Christmas, after the Sunday Christmas service at church.

That afternoon, Alfred and I were sitting at a coffee shop in a mall when all of a sudden, he just broke down crying, in extreme sadness.

It happened so suddenly that I did not know how to react. I thought something had happened. So I kept asking him questions, hoping to get some answers.

However, after talking for a while, I discovered that there really was no trigger that had made him so depressed then. Work might have been a source of stress, but I really did not understand why he had gotten so upset.

All I could do was to sit with him until he felt better.

* * * * * *

Looking back, he was obviously suffering from depression at the time, but I just did not connect the dots. A few days after that incident, he seemed to be back to his normal self. We had discussed the possibility of seeking professional help, but it took a long time before he decided to go.

This was partly due to the fact that he really did not know what was happening to him. We had both attributed it to fatigue and exhaustion, which was partly true.

Back then, we knew little about mental health and seeking help was also perceived as a sign of weakness.

Appendix A: When Love Hurts – By Anna Lam

This is one of the tough realities of living with someone with depression. Family members may notice something is wrong – but until the person acknowledges that there is a problem and agrees to seek counsel, we cannot force them to get professional help.

At the time, I had no understanding of depression at all. Although I had heard of mental illness and have even met people living with depression, I never dreamed that this illness would be inflicted on my family, let alone set off the sequence of events that would turn our world upside down.

In hindsight, I guess there were already tell-tale signs – such as his lack of confidence and being doubtful of himself. He was often withdrawn and quiet as well. His demeanor looked like it was covered with a dark cloud and he seemed very sad.

> I never dreamed that this illness would be inflicted on my family.

This was totally uncharacteristic of Alfred, who is very caring, funny and friendly by nature. He is always encouraging others and willing to lend a hand to those in need. When he sets his mind to do something, he is driven and works diligently with confidence.

But when he became depressed, he would withdraw from his friends and constantly doubt his own abilities, always needing to seek affirmation about his work.

He also suffered from insomnia and a lack of appetite. There was nothing he could do to lighten up his spirit.

I tried to make time to do the kind of things he usually enjoyed doing, and we also took a few vacations together.

Unfortunately, the depression totally robbed him of any interest in life. He was unmotivated to do anything and when he did try, he did not enjoy it at all.

It was clear to me that something was not quite right, but I did not realize that these were the evident signs and symptoms of depression.

I kept concluding that he was merely burned out from ministry and just needed to get more rest.

Beyond Ministry Burnout
However, the trouble that was brewing went much deeper than that. On the outside, our life and marriage looked good, but on the inside lay shambles of hidden problems and complex issues that no one knew about.

Ironically, Alfred's depression was the catalyst that caused all those hidden problems to come to the surface. As his depression deepened, I suddenly felt him trying to push me away rather than letting me in to help him.

At first, I thought it was simply his depression that was causing this shift in our relationship. He was quiet, withdrawn and very irritable around me.

We argued frequently, even over inconsequential things. He came home late very often and avoided conversations with me. As our relationship deteriorated, I started to wonder if there was more to it than meets the eye.

Eventually, my worst fears were confirmed:

Alfred was having an affair.

Appendix A: When Love Hurts – By Anna Lam

Shattered

Like any normal wife, my first reaction was one of shock, anger and betrayal. The hurt and pain were indescribable. My soul was overwhelmed with sorrow and anguish.

While I was trying to cope with Alfred's depression, this final blow came from out of left field and completely brought me down. Discovering the affair just as Alfred's depression was spiralling downwards felt like a double whammy for me.

It felt like I had lost everything. It seemed as if my marriage was ending and my family was falling apart.

* * * * * *

Looking back now, there is good news to share. I have chosen to forgive Alfred, and am pouring my heart and soul into rebuilding my marriage and my life.

The healing journey is long and bumpy, but along the way, I found faith, hope and love in the most unexpected places. I experienced God Himself in the most undesirable circumstances, and He revealed His power through my most helpless and uncertain times.

> I found faith, hope and love in the most unexpected places.

It is truly God's grace that has brought me to where I am today. I am awed and humbled by what He has done in my life and in restoring my marriage.

Every aspect of my life – my home, my church and my marriage – has been made new!

On The Road To Healing
There were two main reasons that made me stay to work things out with my husband.

First, I love Alfred.

It was after much soul-searching that I chose to give our marriage another shot. I was aware that the outcome might not be desirable, but I wanted to give us a second chance if Alfred shared the same desire.

The second reason was our older daughter Taylor. She was only three years old then. When we adopted her, we had promised to love her and be her family.

During Alfred's darkest days, Taylor was the only ray of sunshine for him. I know he loves her very much. If we had decided to split up out of our anger, it would not have been fair to Taylor.

> It was after much soul-searching that I chose to give our marriage another shot.

To be honest, the thought of staying or leaving were equally considered. I knew that each option had its own merits and ultimately, both of us would have to bear the consequences of the decision we made. (As an aside: I personally believe that every couple has their own unique reasons for their choices. In every case, there is really no right or wrong decision.)

Appendix A: When Love Hurts – By Anna Lam

Even before I had made the decision to stay, I had already started seeing a counsellor on my own.

At the time, my emotions were too raw and my mental state was too unstable to even consider my options and make decisions. I knew I needed to clean up my own negative emotions before I could work on my marriage.

Alfred and I both sought counselling separately for a while. We only began marriage counselling after we had decided to stay together. When we made the commitment to stay committed, we knew one thing for sure: things had to change. We did not – could not – remain at status quo.

As we both resolved to work on our marriage, we also recognized that we needed professional help. So we began seeing a counsellor together to rebuild our marriage.

Honest Reckoning

The counselling process was a long process. For about three years, we saw the counsellor together on a regular basis, and thereafter, a few times a year for a "check-up".

It was very emotionally draining. At the time, we were in a broken marriage and what we felt towards each other were not "warm and fuzzy" feelings. Yet the counselling process required us to be downright open in talking about our feelings towards each other!

Alfred would tell me how my words or actions hurt him and made him want to run away from me. Conversely, I would tell him how much I was hurt by the affair.

Confronted by our own weaknesses, there was no way to hide. When we talked about the hurt and pain caused by the other person, conversations could get intense and left us feeling defeated and lost. Often, we were also surprised to find out that our well-intended actions and words had been wrongly perceived and had hurt the other person.

We also talked about how his depression affected us as a couple. We talked about the pain and discouragement we experienced when we had to leave the old church and caused us to lose the community we once knew so well.

Delving into all those issues was often difficult and caused much pain in the core of our being. Many times, we went home after counselling, drained and unable to function. There were definitely moments when I was so discouraged that I felt like quitting.

However painful it was, I saw that Alfred was also making an effort and was committed to this. So that was why I kept telling myself to try just one more time.

I knew it was an essential part of my healing journey too. Of course, an hour-long counselling session once a week would not change anything if we ourselves did not put in the effort and hard work.

Lessons In Progress
What was good about the counselling sessions was that it provided a safe place for us to be vulnerable, open and honest to ourselves and to each other. We had to peel back the layers and masks to really get at the roots. Eventually our relationship did start to improve.

Through this process, I learned several things:

Appendix A: When Love Hurts – By Anna Lam

- **Clarity** – I gained a better understanding of what Alfred was going through living with depression. I am still no expert, but it did give me a better idea of how it has affected his life.

- **Communication** – We told each other honestly about our hurt, our pain and our disappointments. Through this open communication, it made me see my own shortcomings and failures, and how they had also played a role in our broken marriage.

- **Keeping No Records** – In order to rebuild our marriage again, I must keep no record of wrongs. We must work on the marriage with both of us on equal footing.

- **Kindness** – To rebuild a marriage takes patience and kindness. We had been married for 15 years when the hidden problems in our marriage were exposed. During the toughest times in our marriage, we really needed to practice kindness because we could so easily get frustrated and angry with each other.

- **Humility** – The old has to be torn down in order to build something new. In order to start afresh, we needed to put aside our pride and tear down the things that hindered us from being vulnerable to each other in the first place.

- **Lifelong Process** – Rebuilding a broken marriage is a continuous and lifelong process. During the initial recovery period, we went through some really bad days. It took a lot of patience and perseverance, but we managed to press on, hoping that today would be a better day than yesterday.

The New "Normal"
The new "normal" for our marriage is no longer like our old way of life, but there is hope that it can be a deeper and closer relationship. When we decided to stay together, we knew we could not pretend that nothing happened and simply continue living our lives as before.

The hurt and pain must be processed and dealt with. The old "normal" had to go.

In order to establish functionality in our relationship, we needed a new "normal" to start afresh.

This new life meant that we had to acknowledge and accept our past. We also had to understand the weaknesses and shortcomings we both brought into our marriage.

As we have chosen to stay together, we are committed to starting our relationship anew – embracing, loving and accepting each other despite what had happened.

Focusing On The Family
Today Alfred and I are committed to our family and we strive to give the children a normal family life as best as we are able. We do not want Alfred's depression to affect the children. Even at times when he does not feel good,

Appendix A: When Love Hurts – By Anna Lam

we would still try to do "regular" things with the kids – be it taking them out to the playground or the mall, helping them with homework or disciplining them, just like any normal parent would do.

There are still times when Alfred is hit with bouts of depression. It draws him away from being able to enjoy the things he likes to do. Although it can sometimes put a damper in life, he tries really hard to do things with us despite his own condition.

> **In order to establish functionality in our relationship, we needed a new "normal".**

Our older daughter Taylor, notices that daddy is sometimes not a "happy" person. She has always been very observant, and is highly sensitive to other people's mood changes. I would talk to her and explain that no one is happy all the time, but reassure her that daddy loves her just the same.

Now that she is older, she can articulate what she sees and ask me questions. If she notices that Alfred's facial expression seems odd, she would ask her father directly.

We have not discussed in detail with the kids about Alfred's depression as they are too young to comprehend the complexities of the condition. As a family, we are all learning to be more patient, flexible and understanding.

I try to manage my expectations accordingly. On good days, we do more things to enjoy our family time, and on the bad days, we would choose to do less. We had not paid close attention to this before, but now we are much more conscientious about it.

I can usually tell if something is not "right" with Alfred. He would become easily agitated, and even simple things like noise from the children would stress him out and get him really frustrated. Usually at that point, he would rather be alone nor would he have any energy to do anything.

Nowadays, Alfred is more aware when he is vulnerable and we are learning to remove ourselves from potentially stressful situations.

Coping As A Caregiver

I honestly cannot tell you how I managed to survive through the times when Alfred's condition was at its worst all those years ago. It made me feel so helpless and powerless to see him in pain.

The worst period spanned about two to three years. In those days, Alfred completely withdrew himself socially. He suffered from insomnia and could not sleep at night. He was frustrated and did not know how to express his feelings. He built a wall around himself, blocking out everyone, including his own family.

> It made me feel so helpless and powerless to see him in pain.

As it spiralled downward, he began having more suicidal thoughts. I would receive calls from him in the middle of night as he drove around aimlessly, telling me that he could not live any longer, and that he wanted to end his life.

I would stay on the phone and keep talking to him, hoping and praying that he would come home safely.

He felt so much pain that he really could not think straight. He was not able to make decisions and he just lived mindlessly during that time.

> **The only thing I could do was to pray and be there for him.**

My heart ached watching him suffer. So many times I desperately wanted to help him. Many times, when I thought I was trying to help, I actually made things worse.

When a person is suffering from depression, logic and common sense may not always work. I thought I could help Alfred by "analyzing" the situation with him, offering him different options to try, hoping that it would help him come to reasonable conclusions.

More often than not, it actually backfired.

The only thing I could do was pray and be there for him.

Managing My Emotional Health

One thing I have realized is that it is essential for me to get my own emotional health in check. If I am emotionally unstable, it would aggravate his condition further.

After going through so much, I am now way more sensitive to my emotions. I am more conscious about when things do not feel right with me.

Practically, I strive to keep a balance between work and family so that my stress can be better managed.

When I start getting overwhelmed and feel like giving up, I would cut myself some slack, give myself space and quietness so it does not affect Alfred and the kids.

I know I need to be strong for my family, so whenever I feel weak, I would retreat for some alone time.

I find that having time on my own helps me to refocus and get centred again, so I can get up and continue on the journey.

> Having time on my own helps me to refocus and get centred again.

I would also call a friend to talk it out. Having a couple of good friends whom I can confide in has helped me greatly.

When we left the church under those very unpleasant circumstances, I lost my entire faith community in one fell swoop. I am very thankful for my friends and family who have walked with me during these few years and were there to help me get through the most difficult time of my life.

In those few years, I actually experienced my own share of feeling depressed. Though it seemed to be temporary, I caught a glimpse of what depression feels like.

After the affair, I experienced short stints of depression at different times. The feeling of wanting to be alone, loss of appetite, crying uncontrollably, feeling that I am not good for anything, thinking that not being alive is actually

Appendix A: When Love Hurts – By Anna Lam

better than being alive. Often, there was no trigger for those feelings, but they just came. Logic and common sense cannot explain why I felt that way.

Ironically, from those experiences, I gained a better understanding of Alfred's condition.

It is the understanding of how when depression hits, it often is out of his control and not necessarily explainable. I have come to realize that I should not use common sense and logic to "help" Alfred "snap out of it", because it does not work that way.

A Word For Wounded Wives

Depression is an illness that is difficult for outsiders to understand. Watching Alfred suffering from this illness and yet continuously fighting it makes me admire him even more than before.

I know there are days, even now, when he feels so depressed that he wants to give up. I can sense how much pain he is in to be simply "alive".

Yet, despite that, he still tries so hard to hang on with the little strength he has left.

I greatly admire his courage and determination to live another day for us. This constant fighting with his inner self must be excruciating. To everyone who is living with depression, I give them my utmost respect.

For women who have been hurt by their husbands, let me share these words of advice – not as one who knows it all or has overcome everything, but as a fellow sister along the journey:

- **Take your time and do not make hasty decisions out of anger.** There are always choices and there are no guaranteed outcomes. But there are always consequences to every decision.

    Weigh your options carefully. Wait until your emotions have cooled and you are clear-headed before actually making any decisions.

- **No matter what decisions you have made, there will always be critics.** Everyone has an opinion. While it is wise to hear various sides, at the end of the day, you yourself are responsible for your own choices. Do not let others pressure you.

    After you have made your decision, there will be responses from your family and friends. You may even be criticized. My advice is, follow your heart and move on with your life. No one will understand your situation as well as yourself.

    If these friends truly care about you, they will respect your decision and love you just the same. If they choose to distance themselves from you because of your decision, then it is probably not a bad idea to keep that distance anyway.

- **Take care of yourself.** In my time of deep despair, my health was affected. I have now come to realize that you need to take care of both your mental and physical health in order to sustain yourself in the healing process.

Appendix A: When Love Hurts – By Anna Lam

For me, I know my mental stress was affecting my physical health. I had to find ways to reduce my stress. That meant avoiding stressful situations or not overloading myself with too many commitments.

I had to learn to focus my attention on the most important things. It also meant finding ways to relax, exercise and take time off to rest.

- **Talk to someone you can trust.** Having a friend whom you can cry with was a big factor that helped me get through the toughest days.

- **Do not be afraid to ask for help.** Professional counselling is certainly a safe and recommended way to seek help. However, it can be costly.

  If you decide to seek counselling as a couple, be sure to find a counsellor that both of you are comfortable with. For counselling to be helpful, both of you need to be open and honest with your counsellor. If you are reluctant to reveal anything, going to counselling would prove to be useless and pointless in the end.

- **Keep the kids out of it.** If you have children, do not put them between you and your husband. If your husband has hurt you, take it up directly with him – do not take it out on the kids.

* * * * * *

My experience in this journey is but a humbling and growing one. We are still on the journey. Like the title of this book, we lived among the ashes for several years – and yet from among the ashes sprouted new life.

If I had known how serious Alfred's depression was before he spiralled down to the point of utter desperation, we might have been able to reach out for help sooner.

Perhaps then he would not have had to do the things he did in desperate measure, and we would not have had to go through the painful experience of having to leave the church we were pastoring.

> Despite a seemingly hopeless situation, God offered us a lifeline and unexpected hope.

I often worry if Alfred's depression will get worse. I do not know when the next crisis will hit us, but I choose to keep my hopes up. Knowing that "His grace is sufficient for me" gives me the encouragement to press on every day.

My life has undergone significant transformation. During those moments of crisis, I honestly did not know if I would make it. Yet God used different means and brought people (or angels) along the way to help me get through those really dark days.

There is nothing I can boast about my life except my firsthand experiences of God's providence and grace.

With each hardship brought along its lessons learned. Despite a seemingly hopeless situation, God offered us a lifeline and unexpected hope. His grace alone has brought about this redemptive story in our family.

The next chapter is yet unknown, but I do know that however the story develops in the next season, I am already thankful for this enriched life.

APPENDIX B

A Theological Transformation

Daring To Explore My Faith

When I was teaching in the theological seminary years ago, there were two types of conversations that I frequently found myself being drawn into.

The first type of dialogue was with those who felt that they were somehow "unqualified" to participate in theological discussions because they had not attended seminary nor received formal theological education.

I always responded by reminding them that *every* Christian has a set of theological positions, even though they may not necessarily be able to articulate it.

Whether we are consciously aware of it or not, it is our theology that drives our choices and determines our behaviours. The more we are able to reflect and "flesh out" our theology, the better we will be able to understand why we do what we do.

The second type of dialogue took place whenever I raised questions in class and invited the students to discuss some of the commonly held beliefs about what it means to be a Christian. These included questions like:

- Is the gospel simply about "how to go to heaven after you die"?

- Is salvation really only about being saved from going to hell?

- What about people of other religions?

- How should a Christian in the "West" respond in a world of gross economic injustice and oppression, especially when he/she lives in a society which benefits from such inequities?

- Is there a "better" way for the church to respond to the question of homosexuality?

Warning: Danger – "Knowing God" Alert
Too often, when I allow such discussions, a common response I get from people in the church is that such questions are "dangerous".

To which I always point out that *all* theological discussions are "dangerous" by nature!

It is always a dangerous matter to try and "pin down" who God is, what God wants, how God works, and other similar questions within the very restricting limits of our language and our finite minds.

Appendix B: A Theological Transformation

The reality is, how can we possibly fully understand God? It is always dangerous to try and capture what is infinite with tools and means that are finite.

Here is my question in turn:

Which is more dangerous – to keep asking questions and explore, with the assumption that there is more that we do not know and comprehend; or to "nail down" our beliefs within a set of propositions and presumptuously proclaim: "This is all there is to know about God"?

Work In Progress

In the process of engaging in those lively conversations, my own theology has also been shaped and honed.

That said, our theology is always a work in progress, or more accurately, a product of our life journeys. It is shaped by our experiences, the places we have visited, things we have seen, lives that have intersected with ours.

However, unlike most physical journeys, we never get to a place where we can say, "I have arrived."

We are always moving towards the ultimate goal of knowing God personally and intimately.

In 1 Corinthians 13:12, the Scriptures tell us:

> *"For now we see only a reflection as in a mirror;*
> *then we shall see face to face.*
> *Now I know in part; then I shall know fully,*
> *even as I am fully known."*

I also hesitate to call any theology "new" because, to quote Solomon in Ecclesiastes 1:9: "There is nothing new under the sun."

The way I see it, the growth and ongoing development of our theology is very much a part of the work of renewal that God is doing in each of our lives.

RECOMMENDED READING

It is beyond the scope of this book to enter into a lengthy and extended theological discussion. Furthermore, I did not want differences in theological persuasion to distract anyone from identifying with the story of this book.

However, my theology is very much a part of who I am and in many ways, the evolution and growth of my theological outlook mirrors my personal journey as told here in *Among The Ashes*.

The inclusion of this appendix is not so much to lay out my personal itemized "statement of faith", but rather, to broadly chronicle how I arrived at where I am today with regards to what I believe.

To do this would also mean introducing the authors and their books that have influenced me along my journey of theological transformation. They will give you a fairly good idea where I stand theologically.

For those who may be interested in pursuing further reading for your own exploration, these books are a good place to start.

■ **Disappointment With God** – *by Philip Yancey*

When I first became a Christian in the last year of high school, I had a lot of questions about the Christian faith that I did not hear any of my peers asking.

Appendix B: A Theological Transformation

At university, I became one of the leaders in my campus Christian fellowship. Yet I did not feel that I should share my questions and doubts.

I was told that it was quite pointless and ultimately destructive to ask questions that there are no answers to, because in doing so, I may inadvertently "lead others astray", especially those who are young in their faith.

Gradually, I became accustomed to the idea that as part of the "Christian culture", there are questions that you are not supposed to ask.

The first book that gave me a "light bulb" moment was Philip Yancey's *Disappointment With God*.

I was drawn to one particular chapter that was entitled "The Questions No One Asks Aloud".

How fascinating it was to enter a "forbidden domain" – to entertain the thought of asking those questions we were not supposed to ask!

In his book, Yancey also dealt with the tough questions that many have asked in times of pain:

Is God unfair?
Is God silent?
Is God hidden?

To be honest, I did not necessarily find his resolution to the questions very satisfying. But that was not why the book made an impact on me.

I was drawn to the book – not because I was looking for answers, but because for the first time, the book gave me "permission" to ask troubling and challenging questions, even ones that had no simple answers.

■ **In The Name Of Jesus - Reflections On Christian Leadership** – *by Henri Nouwen*

The 1980s and 1990s were the peak of the seeker-sensitive church growth movement. People were flocking to attend conferences held by mega churches.

Books were being published documenting their success stories. Church growth programs were being introduced globally to replicate the successes of the large churches. Big-name pastors were criss-crossing the continent on speaking circuits, addressing sold-out crowds.

I graduated from university in 1988, with the idea of pursuing a career as a pastor. I started attending seminary in 1989, and I distinctly remembered being uncomfortable with what seemed like a "celebrity culture" within a huge multi-million-dollar "industry" (and by that, I mean within the Christian ministry).

Again, I did not feel the freedom to voice those questions because it seemed like all the evangelical churches were heading in that direction.

It was at that time when I was first introduced to the works of Henri Nouwen, in particular, his book *In The Name Of Jesus – Reflections On Christian Leadership*.

In his book, Nouwen articulated the kind of faith and ministry style that I was secretly longing for – kinder, more humble, less "corporate" and more about community, less "pep talk" and more about silence, more about prayer.

Incidentally, it was not until later that I learned that Henri Nouwen also suffered from depression. It turned out that my therapist also knew him personally as a friend.

Appendix B: A Theological Transformation

■ **A Long Obedience In The Same Direction – Discipleship In An Instant Society –** *by Eugene Peterson*
During my years in seminary, another author who further shaped my preference for a more reflective approach to faith was Eugene Peterson.

He took a small collection of psalms and wrote about something basic: discipleship. His writing felt much more "real and authentic", compared to the "culture of success" that was so popular at the time.

Reading both Nouwen and Peterson affirmed within me a conviction that I still hold dear to my heart today: *there ought to be a difference between how companies like Coca Cola and the church define and measure "success"!*

■ **A New Kind Of Christian; A Generous Orthodoxy; A New Kind Of Christianity –** *all by Brian McLaren*
As we entered the new millennium, "seeker-sensitive church growth" gave way to "post-modernism" as the trendy topic for the day among churches.

Everywhere I turned, it seemed like there was another workshop and another conference being held to warn the church of this insidious enemy called "post-modernism".

Once again, I found myself in the familiar position of secretly wrestling with questions of faith and questioning what it was that lay at the heart of Christianity.

While the general church at large was on "high alert" against the dangers of post-modernism, I found myself identifying with the issues that the post-modern movement was raising:

- Questioning the "institutional-focused" approach to Western Evangelical Christianity
- Raising issues of environmental concerns and creation stewardship
- Challenging the "traditional" understanding of what it means to be "saved"
- Opening doors of dialogue and partnership with those of different faith backgrounds to build God's Kingdom on earth by speaking out against injustice, raising awareness of global issues, caring for the poor, etc.

In an atmosphere where the "battle lines" were drawn between the "new" and the "old", where intolerance and arrogance were mistaken for faithfulness and confidence, I discovered Brian McLaren.

His books not only articulated many of the views which I identified with, but more importantly, he showed me that *how* we articulate our faith is just as important as the actual content of our beliefs.

He demonstrated that it is possible – *crucial*, in fact – that we learn to communicate matters of faith and doctrines in a manner that invites keen dialogue and discussion, with a genuine open-mindedness, graciousness and humility that is reflective of the character of Christ.

For anyone wanting to get a handle on the post-modern approach to the Christian faith, Brian McLaren's books are a great place to begin.

Appendix B: A Theological Transformation

■ Surprised By Hope – Rethinking Heaven, The Resurrection And The Mission Of The Church – *by N. T. Wright*

Even as a pastor myself, I felt that it was not enough that I could articulate what I was thinking and believing. I also needed to be able to engage Scripture and use that as the shared platform for discussion.

That is where N. T. (Nicholas Thomas) Wright's writings became extremely helpful.

Wright is widely acclaimed as one of the most prolific biblical scholars of our generation. In scholarly fashion, his book argued for a re-examination and a different understanding of the fundamentals of the Christian faith, such as the meaning of the gospel, the nature of salvation, the mission of the church, etc.

He built his case exclusively from a disciplined, historical interpretation of Scriptures, which helps one to systematically follow his train of thought.

Between McLaren and Wright, I found my model of what biblical scholarship should look like: disciplined and careful, yet gracious and humble.

* * * * * *

This, then, is a brief account of how I got to where I am today theologically.

It is my belief that the gospel is not about going to heaven after we die, but *bringing God's Kingdom to earth while we live.*

It is my belief that salvation is not just about ensuring the eternal destination of our souls, but *the redemption and restoration of God's entire creation.*

It is my belief that the church is not merely a religious organization that is tasked with recruiting people into the Christian religion, but *a community commissioned to go out into the world to show who Jesus is.*

As I journey forward, I have no doubt that my faith and my theology will continue to grow and evolve.

To me, engaging in rethinking my faith and theology is all part of the process of renewal, the fermenting of this "new wine" that Jesus talked about.

As I mentioned in Chapter Six, I believe our challenge as a church today is to become the kind of "new wineskin" that is strong enough to protect the new wine, yet flexible enough to allow for its continuous growth and expansion.

* * * * * *

One of the recurring themes that flows through the entire biblical narrative is how God surprises His people with the depth and breadth of His love.

In the Old Testament, the prophet Jonah could not imagine a God who would be compassionate towards the idolatrous people of Assyria and its capital city, Nineveh.

Similarly, in the New Testament, the church had to come to grips with the idea that God's love does extend beyond the Jews to the Gentiles, and that one does not need to undergo circumcision to qualify for God's love.

Appendix B: A Theological Transformation

In Acts 10, God also challenged Peter with a vision to show him that He does not operate by rote traditions and legalistic rules as imposed by the Pharisees.

In the same way, I believe God continues to challenge us to see Him afresh today.

Like Peter, are we willing to see Him with new eyes and grow with an ever-expanding vision of who God is? Are we willing to be stretched in our understanding of how He works, and let Him surprise us with the depth and breadth of His love?

As you embark on your own journey of exploring your faith, my prayer is that your goal is not simply to have a theology that is better articulated or more academically sophisticated.

Instead, may your journey lead you to a place where you are awed by His glory and greatness – and amazed by His grace and compassion towards us.

In discovering Him afresh, may we gratefullly proclaim along with the psalmist in Psalm 8:

> *"When I consider Your heavens,*
> *the work of Your fingers,*
> *the moon and the stars,*
> *which You have set in place,*
> *what is man that You are mindful of him,*
> *the son of man that You care for him?"*

APPENDIX C

Getting The Help You Need

Daring To Ask For Assistance

Type the word "Depression" into a Google search, and you will get over 64 million results in less than a second. Evidently, there is no lack of information available out there. So why is it that for so many who suffer from depression – as well as those who are close to them – still struggle with a pervasive sense of "helplessness" while trying to cope with the illness?

My own experience with depression has taught me that information itself is not enough. When someone is going through depression, he or she needs help from a network of individuals as well as a strategy that often includes radical lifestyle changes.

This book is not meant to be a comprehensive resource book for all topics related to depression. However, I would like to share what I have found helpful in my own journey.

Neither do I claim the resources listed in this appendix as the "best available". My intention is only to share with you the different kinds of assistance that contributed to my own journey of recovery and give you a sense of the helpful "ingredients" needed for an effective coping and/or treatment strategy for someone who has depression.

(NB: The resources below are not listed in any particular order. As I live in Toronto, most of the organizations I dealt with are based locally.)

Ingredient #1: Accurate Information
While there is a wealth of information available out there, there is also a lot of "misinformation", not just in the public realm, but particularly within the church.

From talking with various Christians, I encountered many theories/teachings that link depression to what I call "pseudo-spiritual" causes.

They claim that depression is the result of demonic influences; or that depression is the symptom of a weak faith; or that one can worship/pray/meditate/fast oneself out from depression, and so on.

The first step towards dealing with any problem is to clearly understand what you are dealing with. That means getting accurate information.

I have personally found the information on this website **www.depressionhurts.ca** to be very helpful. It is presented clearly and easy to access.

Furthermore, there is also a practical section written for friends and family of people suffering from depression and advising them on how they can help.

Ingredient #2: Medical Advice

It is important to speak with your doctor about what you are feeling because he or she can perform tests to rule out other possibilities that may be causing your symptoms.

For example, thyroid problems have been known to cause symptoms of fatigue, depression and anxiety.

By telling your family doctor, he or she can perform a complete physical examination to rule out medical issues.

Your doctor should also be familiar with professionally accepted diagnostic criteria and know how to ascertain whether you are indeed suffering from depression.

There are two further benefits from seeing your family doctor that you cannot get from a counsellor or therapist.

First, your doctor can prescribe some antidepressant medication for you if necessary.

Secondly, depending on the severity and complexity of your symptoms, your family doctor can also refer you to a psychiatrist who is trained to treat mental, emotional and behavioural disorders.

In Canada, you can only see a specialist, such as a psychiatrist, upon a referral from a family doctor.

Ingredient #3: Antidepressant Medication

In my own experience, when I revealed to my friends and family that my doctor had prescribed antidepressant medication, I was not prepared for the reactions I received from well-meaning individuals.

Some practically pleaded with me not to take it at all. They told me that once I started medication, I would have to take it for the rest of my life (which is not true). Some warned me that it would cause all kinds of unwanted side effects (it did not, in my case). Others even said that the medication would change my personality (again, not true).

I am not qualified to discuss the risks and benefits of the different antidepressant medications available today. For that same reason, I also hesitate to disclose the name of the medication that I took. Just because it worked very well for me without any major side effects does not mean it is for everyone. Depending on your own body and brain chemistry, there may well be another medication that is more suitable for you.

However, when people ask me about my experiences with antidepressants, I must always mention one thing:

Antidepressant medication is not a "happy pill". It will not automatically stop all symptoms of depression the same way Benadryl stops an allergic reaction.

When I started taking antidepressants, it basically did two things for me: first, it elevated the "floor" of my despair so that my valleys of sadness did not sink as deep.

Secondly, I felt more "clear-headed" or rational so that I could process the information and advice my therapist was giving to me. Those two effects combined made it possible for counselling to do its work.

The best advice I can share with anyone who has been prescribed antidepressant medication is what my own doctor had said to me:

"There is nothing heroic or brave about refusing to take medication. If you come to my office with an infection and

Appendix C: Getting The Help You Need

I prescribe an antibiotic for you, chances are, you will not go through the same thought process about whether you should take it or not."

Listen carefully to your doctor.

Seek a second opinion if you feel it is necessary.

By all means, ask as many questions as you want about the medication.

However, if there is one thing NOT to do, it is this: do not set up an arbitrary "bottom line" and shortchange yourself by declaring, "I will do everything EXCEPT take medication to deal with my depression."

Ingredient #4: Counselling Therapy

This is another critical element of an effective treatment strategy for depression. Many have asked: "What should I look for in a counsellor or therapist?"

That question is tremendously difficult to answer because there are so many factors that can determine whether you are a "good match" for any given counsellor.

I have listed some questions below that you may want to ask when looking for a counsellor:

1. Do I feel more comfortable working with a male or female counsellor?

This is entirely up to you. I have spoken to some men who prefer a female counsellor. Conversely, I have met women who will absolutely not consider a male counsellor. There are some for whom it does not matter. It all depends on your personal comfort level.

2. Do I only want to see a Christian counsellor?

Again, this is a question of individual preference. When I was looking for a counsellor, this was not an absolute must for me. In fact, in some respects, I actually preferred to see a non-Christian counsellor because after spending so many years in the church community, I wanted someone who could offer me a fresh point of view.

I ended up seeing a therapist who turned out to be a Christian. I chose her because she was first and foremost an excellent professional, rather than on the basis of her faith or religion.

My approach to this question can be summarized this way: Just because you are a Christian does not mean you should ONLY seek help from a Christian counsellor.

Conversely, just because a counsellor is a Christian does not automatically mean he or she is right for you.

3. What is the counsellor's preferred approach to therapy?

Some counsellors specialize in Emotion-Focused Therapy. Some prefer a Cognitive-Behavioural approach. Some are more explicitly faith-based in their counselling.

This is an important question to raise at the initial consultation with a potential counsellor because if you do not resonate with the counsellor's basic approach, chances are, he or she is not the right one for you.

Another important point to note is that you are not "committed" or "locked in" to any particular counsellor. You always have the freedom to stop seeing him or her if you no longer find it to be the right fit.

Appendix C: Getting The Help You Need

4. Can I afford this person?
Counselling is expensive. At the time I am writing this book, professional counselling fees in Toronto range from $100 to $150 per hour.

Some counsellors may consider adjusting his or her rates depending on the client's financial situation.

Some agencies also offer counselling on a sliding scale fee based on the client's income. Some organizations in the community offer funded counselling services for free.

A number of pastors have asked me what their church can do to support those suffering from depression.

If I may offer a suggestion for leaders to consider: one of the most practical things a church can do is to set a budget to help individuals/families who need counselling but cannot afford it on their own.

For myself, I ended up seeing Diane Marshall at the Institute of Family Living (**www.ifl.on.ca,** *tel: 416-487-3613*). Besides the fact that Diane is an excellent and experienced counsellor, I chose the Institute of Family Living because they take a multi-discipline approach to counselling.

Depression is not an illness that happens in isolation. It touches all aspects of the person's life and often leads to other struggles such as addiction, marital problems, employment issues and so on. The fact that the Institute of Family Living has counsellors who specialize in these different issues was an important factor for me.

Additionally, I have found the following organizations in Toronto to be helpful and have volunteered with them. They are excellent resources and offer quality programs and services, not only for those suffering from mental illnesses but also for the families involved:

- Hong Fook Mental Health Association (**www.hongfook.ca**)

- Canadian Mental Health Association – York Region (**www.cmha-yr.on.ca**)

- Family Services of York Region (**www.fsyr.ca**) offer counselling services with fees based on a sliding scale.

NOTES

NOTES

www.ingramcontent.com/pod-product-compliance
Lightning Source LLC
Chambersburg PA
CBHW062107080426
42734CB00012B/2782